A
COLLISION OF
TRUTHS

A
COLLISION OF
TRUTHS

A Life in Conflict with a Cherished Faith

Robert Y. Ellis

iUniverse, Inc.
New York Bloomington Shanghai

A Collision of Truths
A Life in Conflict with a Cherished Faith

iUniverse books may be ordered through booksellers or by contacting:

iUniverse
1663 Liberty Drive
Bloomington, IN 47403
www.iuniverse.com
1-800-Authors (1-800-288-4677)

Because of the dynamic nature of the Internet, any Web addresses or links contained in this book may have changed since publication and may no longer be valid.

ISBN: 978-0-595-45627-7 (pbk)
ISBN: 978-0-595-70520-7 (cloth)
ISBN: 978-0-595-89928-9 (ebk)

Printed in the United States of America

The views expressed in this work are solely those of the author and do not necessarily reflect the views of the publisher, and the publisher hereby disclaims any responsibility for them.

Cover: The photograph on the cover shows the reflection of The First Church of Christ, Scientist edifice in the reflecting pool at the Christian Science Church Center, Boston.

Photographs by Jeph Ellis Image Maker

To my wife, Barbara, and
Carly, Jeff, and Magda.
Their very existence
and constant support
made this story possible.

CONTENTS

Part II

PREFACE

I was born by cesarean section in 1934 at the Flower Fifth Avenue Hospital in Manhattan. What makes this remarkable is the fact that my mother, Katherine Ellis, was a devout Christian Scientist. Christian Scientists were renowned for not going to doctors or hospitals. My birth also was remarkable because my mother had been told that she could not have children. So, regardless of how and where I was born, my conception and birth were what some might have called a miracle. But, to my mother my birth was nothing more than a Christian Science demonstration of what she considered to be the "absolute truth of being." There are no miracles in Christian Science. Instead, healings are considered *demonstrations* of the healing power of God as taught in Christian Science.

From the earliest of days, my mother taught me how Christian Science worked. I learned that God was not a person or a being up in heaven. Rather, God was Mind, Principle, Life, Spirit, Soul, Truth, and Love. Every Christian Scientist learns that those are the seven synonyms for God. I learned that Jesus was able to heal because he understood those synonyms. And he understood that God was perfect. Since God was perfect and infinite, it followed that God's entire creation was perfect. That meant that we were perfect, even if our limited mortal vision kept us from seeing that perfection. As children of God, no matter what our condition seemed to be, we were without blemish.

My mother and my Sunday school teachers also taught me that Jesus had a system that he used for healing, which he taught his disciples. His system was very simple in principle. He beheld God's perfect man where others beheld a leper. Think of it. Jesus literally saw that individual in his perfect godlike state. And Jesus's perfect discernment transformed that leper into a whole person. Jesus could transform every wrong he saw into good. He could quell the storm, heal the sick, and raise the dead. His disciples and Paul, who never knew Jesus, also understood this system; that is why they were able to heal people. I would be able to do so also, if I could only learn to understand as Jesus understood.

According to my teachers, this system was a science. That's why our religion was called Christian Science. However, unlike traditional science, which requires proof of its theories in the laboratory, proof of the efficacy of Christian Science is found in the thousands of healings or demonstrations that have been published in the monthly *Christian Science Journal* and the weekly *Christian Science Sentinel* and recorded in the Christian Science Archives in Boston.

As a little boy living in a home filled with love, I remember a sense of warmth. The only discord I experienced in those earlier years came from a feeling of separateness from my friends, none of whom were Christian Scientists. But Christian Science was, in my mother's eyes, the absolute truth or science of being. And I, her very special only child, often imagined in my early years that I was destined to become an important person in the Christian Science movement—certainly a Christian Science practitioner, and perhaps a member of the board of directors in Boston, a position that would have marked the epitome of success.

My father, James Ellis, was raised in Christian Science but had rejected it before he met and married my mother. When I was young, he never instructed me per se as to what his beliefs were. However, when I was in grammar school he made me stand up to the principal of my school because she had directed that all the boys wear a dress shirt and necktie to school. My father felt that my principle was requiring a school uniform, typical of what the Catholic kids wore to their parochial schools. This, he believed, was a violation of the separation of church and state clause of the First Amendment of the U.S. Constitution.

Then, at the height of McCarthyism, and just before I entered my sophomore year of high school, my father and mother personally experienced what are now known as the Peekskill Riots. They saw thousands of people beaten because of their political beliefs. The riots enraged my father. He had only completed a high school education, but that didn't stop him from being an ardent student of the writings of Tom Paine. He firmly believed in the principles enunciated in the Bill of Rights of the United States Constitution. He quickly joined the executive board of the Westchester Committee for Human Rights. He also formed and became president of the Yonkers Committee for Peace. He fought several battles with local authorities over the right of organizations to hold meetings in public places. The American Civil Liberties Union carried one of his battles to the Supreme Court of the United States. My father and I traveled to Washington DC to watch as the case was argued. Watching those nine justices preside over my father's case was a very moving experience for me. I suspect that this experience caused me to consider going to law school.

My father was not a religious person in the normal sense of the word. Once, when I questioned him, my father told me that he was an agnostic. However, he stood up for the ideals upon which our nation was founded with what I thought was a kind of religious fervor—so much so that I often asked myself, "What is religion?"

I marvel to this day that until long after I left their household, I was mostly unaware of any dissension between my parents about religious matters. I had married Barbara Wemyss;[1] she was a Christian Scientist, as were her parents. Barbara and I invited my parents to see our new home. By this time I had graduated from law school, and my father had thought that I would follow the path he hoped for—championing civil rights in the courts. Instead, I had left the law, become a staff writer for the *Christian Science Monitor,* and become an active member of our local Christian Science church.

The minute my parents entered our house, Barbara and I sensed a feeling of tension. In the middle of dinner, my father declared he couldn't stand the Christian Science atmosphere of our home, got up from the table, left our house, and went out into the night even though it was pouring rain. I realized for the first time how frustrated and angry he must have felt over the religious and career courses I had taken. He must have felt that he had lost out to our world of Christian Science. Looking back, I see how religious groups can, however unwittingly, exclude people—even their own family members.

My father was murdered in 1972. He and I were terribly estranged by that time. He suffered a violent death at the hands of two thieves whom he had let into Broadway Carpet Service at 1968 Amsterdam Avenue in Harlem, in New York City, after he had locked the place up for the night. Broadway Carpet was the last white-owned business in the neighborhood. He was memorialized at a local church service, which was attended by hundreds of his black neighbors and friends.

I had a difficult time dealing with his murder then. I had an extremely difficult time writing about it many years later—it was as though I was reliving the tragedy with the same tears coming to my eyes.

I leaned heavily on God after my father's murder. So did my mother. It greatly helped us cope. "Trust" is an important word in Christian Science. It shows up seventy times in Mary Baker Eddy's[2] writings. One learns to trust God in all things and through all things. One leans on God. One lets God act through oneself. So my family trusted, and we moved on. I became very active in our local Christian Science church—ushering, serving on the executive board, and serving as First Reader. The height of my devotion to Christian Science occurred one Sunday morning when I was conducting a service in our Christian Science

---

1.   Pronounced Weems
2.   The founder of Christian Science.

branch church in Rockport, Massachusetts and I experienced what I sometimes describe as an epiphany.

Then I discovered the worlds of physics, cosmology, and psychology, which appeared to be about as far removed from Christian Science as could be possible.

I read Carl Jung's autobiography followed by biographies of Albert Einstein[3] and Niels Bohr.[4] I was fascinated by Jung's description of what he called "synchronicity," which he thought might be the manifestation of a universal "a-causal connecting principle." Einstein had brought the twentieth century into the world of relativity. Bohr had revolutionized scientific thinking in the world of quantum theory. As I read these books and many more, I found myself feeling like a fly on the wall as I "listened" to these great theorists reason through to conclusions that revolutionized scientific thinking. Twentieth century scientists seemed to me to have discovered that what mankind had always thought was the truth about matter was quite incorrect and quite misleading—a conclusion easily understood by a Christian Scientist. Interpretations of recent findings have come to the point where a few scientists are beginning to speculate on God's place, if any, in a fourteen-billion-year-old universe—attempting, in fact, to define God.

"How can you find those books you're reading so interesting?" my mother once asked me. "All one needs to know about reality is contained in these books," she said as she pointed to her *Science and Health* by Mary Baker Eddy and her King James Version of the Bible. She believed emphatically that a complete statement of the truth or the science of being was contained in the teachings of Christian Science. All one needed to understand was what God is and what man's relationship to God is.

But I found myself inexplicably drawn into this scientific world. It was heady stuff. I spent so much time trying to understand quantum theory's suggestion that a conscious connectedness exists throughout this universe of ours. I wanted to grasp Einstein's theory of general relativity, which describes a geometry of space-time in which we live and of which we all are a part, and I wanted to comprehend the eleven-dimensional string theory, which brings us to the vibrations of the universe to which we all, from the most infinitesimal to the most grand, must listen. I couldn't explain it to my mother. I can't explain it to myself, nor to my wife, nor to most of my friends. Why has this happened to me? Once, while attending a service, I inadvertently sighed audibly. One of my fellow parishioners told me she heard it. She recognized that I seemed to be tired of all the old plati-

---

3.   *Subtle is the Lord, The Science and the Life of Albert Einstein* by Abraham Pais
4.   *Niels Bohr's Times, In Physics, Philosophy, And Polity* by Abraham Pais

tudes I had heard in so many Christian Science services. I apologized profusely, and then I told her that I wished there were some kind of room in our organization for the exploration of new ideas. She had no answer for me.

Strangely, looking at the cosmos through these studies has also caused me to appreciate all manifestations of life on this Earth of ours. I find myself marveling at a spider as she crawls across my bedroom ceiling, or in awe of my cat's ability to leap effortlessly and perfectly onto my kitchen counter. Then there's the question "What *is* music?" I know it is made up of sounds produced by various combinations of notes sounded by various and sundry instruments or voices. But what is it? Why does it enthrall? I sometimes wonder if, in the end, music is the language of God.

My mother remained in my life for many years after my father's death. We were very close. She died three months prior to her ninety-fifth birthday. I had always expected her to die a peaceful death, perhaps relaxing in her favorite armchair with a copy of *Science and Health* in her lap. But no. She suffered through six months of excruciatingly painful cancer. What did a loving, caring Christian Science God have to say about that? Nothing, so far as I could see.

But a scintilla of the understanding I gained in Christian Science lingers. I still lean on what I tend to define as Intelligence, or Carl Jung's "a-causal connecting principle." And I believe that with the explosion of scientific discoveries taking place these days, we are on the brink of discovering scientifically that timeless, universal intelligence is at work and available to us ordinary folk. It explains the healing, transcendent, and creative in our lives. This concept, for me, is profoundly stimulating and liberating. And it exists completely outside of rigid religious dogma, which, in my opinion, insulates us from our fellow man and keeps us from knowing each other.

During the past thirty years, I've voraciously explored the sciences and philosophies. If recent decades of evolution in scientific and religious conclusions are an example, I can only marvel at the possibilities for the future. Great strides are going to be made. Points of view will be forced to change, and cherished beliefs will be severely challenged.

ACKNOWLEDGMENTS

Writing a memoir about one's own life and especially about one's most cherished beliefs and the subsequent unraveling of those beliefs is not an easy task. Steven C. Law, a writer, editor, and Congregational minister, told me I should write this memoir and how to do it. He held my hand through my ten-year endeavor.

The evolution of my thought started some thirty years ago when Ned Bright, my Swarthmore College roommate, showed me the first of an innumerable number of books and treatises regarding the physical and mental sciences. Over time, I consumed each of them. And he fed me many more titles as the years went by. Westin Boer, writer and deep thinker, read my manuscript, and during many a bike ride, questioned my thought processes. Judy Barrett, English grammarian extraordinaire, held my feet to the fire regarding both my prose and my reasoning. Peter Minasian, marketing and communications consultant, after reading my manuscript, offered to help me bring this book to you, the reader. These are only five of so many people who have offered so much helpful advice and to whom I am very grateful.

In most cases I have changed the names of the players in *A Collision of Truths*—childhood and adult friends and acquaintances, police officers, doctors, nurses, and all others who are a part of what follows. The names of historical figures, family members, relatives, and those who are very close to me are accurate. No matter the angst some of us may have experienced, every individual who is a part of this narrative was and still is important to my continuing journey.

You are a child of the universe,
No less than the trees and the stars: …
And whether or not it is clear to you,
No doubt the universe is unfolding as it should.

Max Ehrmann's *Desiderata*

PART I

BOOKS

In 1938, during the Great Depression, I was four years old and the only child of Mary Katherine and James Rains Ellis. We lived in a small, two-story clapboard house with a spacious yard in a nice neighborhood in Bryn Mawr, a part of Yonkers that lies just outside New York City. While my father was away at work in the city, my mother took care of our home and watched over me.

One morning, after washing the dishes, she brought three books out to our back porch where I played with my toys. One of the books was the Bible. The second was *Science and Health with Key to the Scriptures* by Mary Baker Eddy. They were bound in leather, printed on onionskin paper, and had a special, pleasant odor, which spoke to me of elegance and maybe a little mystery. The third book looked like a small magazine; it was titled the *Christian Science Quarterly*.

On this morning, the book my mother was reading came to rest in her lap. Her brow was slightly furrowed, but she wore a gentle smile. She appeared to be looking at nothing. I asked her what she was doing. But she only continued to look off into the distance.

My mother probably was the most important person in my life. In a way she must have seemed larger-than-life to me even though she stood only four feet ten inches tall. I looked at her now with her black hair trimmed just below her ears and with bangs over her forehead. She had blue eyes just like me. She was slender in the waist but had a full figure.

I asked her again: "What are you doing, Mommy?"

"What, dear?" she asked as she turned her gaze in my direction. Her eyes sparkled as she focused on me. She smiled and said, "I'm studying my weekly lesson."

She showed me her Bible and *Science and Health,* which had thin, flat springy pieces of metal with numbered tabs on their ends sticking out from the pages. The tabs indicated in what order she should read the pages. She explained, "So I read the passages in the Bible that are spelled out in the *Quarterly*, and then I read passages in *Science and Health,* which help me get a clearer understanding of the Bible passages. Just now, I was thinking about one of the passages in the Bible."

She said there were people all over the world just like her who studied the Bible every morning. They then picked up *Science and Health* and studied it. She told me that *Science and Health* explained the Bible. "Studying Science and Health helps me get a clearer understanding of the Bible," she said. She liked that expression "clearer understanding." She often was looking for a clearer understanding of things, she would tell me.

"Where does the *Quarterly* come from?" I asked.

"It's published by the Mother Church, and it tells me what passages to read each week in the Bible and *Science and Health*."

"Oh. What's the Mother Church?"

"It's in Boston where Christian Science was founded by Mary Baker Eddy."

"Oh. Who's Mary Baker Eddy?"

"She's a very important person who was once extremely ill and got better because she studied the Bible. The doctors couldn't help her, but the Bible did. She wrote *Science and Health* so people like you and me could gain an understanding of how true healing takes place."

"How does it work?" I asked.

"Well that's very difficult to explain, Bobby, especially at your age. It's really a lifelong search. Mrs. Eddy had a sudden inspiration, which healed her. But it took her a long time to figure out just what happened. It required a lot of studying and what I like to call mental work. That's why I study every day, and that's why I take you to Sunday school. That way, when you're old enough, you'll be able to get some sense of how it works, and to make it your own understanding. It's quite thrilling when ideas come to you and suddenly open the door to a new light, a new understanding. That's what I was doing just now—thinking things through until I could get an understanding of what I had just read."

I didn't really understand what she was saying at the time. But this was how she taught me throughout my childhood. And it stuck with me. I've often found myself staring into space, quietly looking for a new understanding.

My mother planned her days so she could do her studying and mental work every morning. In wintertime, the porch was enclosed with storm windows, which let the sunlight pour in, warming the space. In summer, the glass was removed, and screens were installed to allow air to circulate. Whatever the season, she sat on that porch and studied, except on Sunday mornings, when she took me in hand to go to church and Sunday school.

I remember those hours my mother and I spent on that porch as being wonderfully warm. The sun pouring in had a lot to do with it. But my mother's sense of peace also filled the room. I suppose I got bored at times. But I had my toys. And my mother's quiet time with her books had a comforting, warming effect on me.

SUNDAY SCHOOL

My mom told me that when I was really little, before we moved to Bryn Mawr, I went to the nursery in the church she attended near our home on 104th Street in Manhattan.

But now, she took me to Sunday school in the Christian Science Church in Bronxville. My mother attended a service upstairs while I was in a class downstairs. There were four boys and girls my age. We learned all about Daniel and how God took care of him in the lions' den. We were told that God took care of Moses when he was a baby boy and he was found floating in the rushes by the Pharaoh's daughter. We then learned that Moses grew up and led the Jews to freedom, and that God sent manna from heaven and made water come out of a rock so Moses and his followers could eat and drink. We also learned that God took care of Joseph after his brothers sold him into slavery.

"Just like your mother takes care of you, that's how God takes care of all of us," our teacher said.

Our teacher read these Bible stories to us. She also had us look at picture books, which told the same stories, and she had coloring books that we could fill in with crayons. That way, we learned the stories even though we couldn't yet read.

Sunday school was kind of fun. I got to be with the other kids for awhile. But I hated getting dressed for Sunday school. My mother made me wear a scratchy, wool, tweed suit. It was so scratchy that I wore my pajama bottoms under the pants so it wouldn't itch so much. She also made me wear a white dress shirt and tie. But then everybody dressed very formally for church. The ushers all wore black suits with tails. Mom said they were "mourning suits." So I figured these men always wore their suits in the morning. My father never wore such a thing, though. He wore a regular suit to work every morning.

My mother told me that my father had once been a Christian Scientist, but he wasn't anymore. He never dressed up on Sundays because he always stayed at home and read the paper while we went to church—a constant reminder that there was a difference of belief in our home.

CONTRAPTIONS

One sunny, early spring Sunday morning in 1940, my father came into my bedroom.

"Get up, Bobby. You're skipping Sunday school today. We're going downtown. There's something I want you to see."

I had just turned six years old. We had recently moved from Bryn Mawr to our new home in a two-family house on the corner of Spencer Avenue and 263rd Street in Riverdale in the Bronx.

I leaped out of bed and got dressed as quickly as I could. Then, my parents and I walked down Spencer Avenue and two blocks over to the Broadway bus, which took us down to the IRT subway at 242nd Street. We climbed the stairs to the elevated station and got on the last car of the train that was waiting for us.

As the train started moving, my father took my hand. We walked through seven cars until we got to the front. He positioned us so we were standing with our noses practically touching the glass of the front door. That way, we could see everything the engineer was seeing. He was sitting to our right in his little cubicle. My mother sat on one of the seats with the other passengers. I looked up at my dad. My chin was just above the windowsill. He was about one and a half feet taller than I was. His blue eyes stared intently out the window.

I looked at the engineer and saw him moving a lever.

"He controls our speed with that lever," my father said. "Watch when we come to the next stop. You'll see how the train slows down as he moves it. Then when we leave, watch how he moves it in the opposite direction to make the train speed up."

After the Dykeman Street station, the train went underground. It was dark and kind of mysterious in the tunnel as blurry lights sped by.

"Watch the signal lights," my dad said. "See that green light we're approaching? That tells the engineer he can go fast. But you watch. As we approach a station, the light will be yellow. That'll tell him he needs to slow down."

Sure enough, as we approached the next station there was a yellow light. The engineer began to move his lever, and the train slowed down. It was really neat the way my father knew so much. I wondered if there was anything he didn't know.

Soon we came to the 157th Street Station in Harlem where I knew Dad got off to go to work at his carpet cleaning factory every day, sometimes even on Sundays. Dad walked with a limp because a large carpet cleaning machine had fallen on his right ankle while he was helping to get the machine installed. The break never healed properly. Still, even with a bad ankle and a slim physique, he easily lifted large rolls of carpet.

After thirty minutes, we arrived at Times Square. Dad took my hand and led us up the stairs and out into the daylight. We walked perhaps a block before entering a restaurant where my father had me sit facing the front.

"Now then," he said with a big grin on his face. "Tell me if you can see why I brought you here."

I looked around and saw sights familiar to every restaurant I had ever been in: people sitting at other tables and on swivel stools at a counter; waitresses taking orders, bringing food and coffee, and clearing tables. Then my eyes settled on a round machine in the front window. The machine was a lot taller than I was, and it was wider than our table. It looked sort of like a very large, tiered wedding cake.

Near the top, two faucets with spouts pointing down extended over a slowly rotating cooking surface, which was heated from beneath by blue gas flames. The first faucet squirted what looked like oil onto the moving shelf. Then, right after that, the second faucet squirted out some yellow goo. About halfway around, a spatula shot out from the center of the machine under the partially cooked goo and flipped it over. The shelf continued moving, and just before it got back to the faucets, another spatula flipped the fully cooked goo off onto a big heated tray.

"What do you think of that?" my father asked. "Isn't that something?"

"Yeah," I said. I still was unsure about what I was looking at. I wondered if it was one of his latest contraptions.

My father was always building contraptions. He built one of the first I ever saw when we lived in Bryn Mawr. He mounted some corrugated tin on top of a kerosene space heater and onto the hood of his car. The tin directed the heat into the engine area and kept the oil thin enough for the engine to turn over on cold winter mornings. His heater worked well for about a week—until it burned down our detached garage and burned up his car.

Before I was born, he had made a portable shower complete with curtain, out of tubing and rubber hoses. A traveling salesman could pack the shower in his suitcase so he could take a shower in his hotel room, which in those days usually only had a bathtub. And just after we moved into our Spencer Avenue house, he spent hours and hours building a folding door for our closet. He tried to get patents for these and many other inventions, but someone else always got there before him.

When the waitress came to our table, my father spoke for us all.

"We'll each have an order of pancakes with bacon and lots of butter and syrup. We'll also have coffee—and a glass of milk for our son, please."

The waitress went to the machine, removed some of the cooked goo, and divided it onto three plates. She then went behind the counter and put bacon on the plates. She put the plates on a tray along with some syrup, butter, two cups of coffee, and my milk, and she brought it to our table.

"Imagine that," my father said as he slathered butter and syrup over his pancakes, speared a big bite with his fork, and held the fork in front of his mouth, "an automatic pancake making machine. Quite something, isn't it?"

"Yeah," I said as my mother and I bit into our pancakes.

Soon our plates were clean, and the waitress cleared them away. My father sat with his left elbow on the table and his chin in his hand. "You know, I knew the man who made that machine," he said.

"You did?" So this wasn't one of Dad's contraptions.

Mother watched the two of us with a benign smile on her face. Daddy frequently worked seven days. Little excursions like this one with the three of us together were rare.

"Let's see," my father continued. "This is 1940, so it must have been about twelve or thirteen years ago—in 1927 or '28—before the crash. The inventor expected to sell these machines to restaurants all over the city and across the country. He got my mother—your grandmother—and a lot of other people to loan him money so he could build it. My mother expected that he would sell lots of pancake machines and end up paying everybody back, plus a lot more."

He removed his chin from his hand and looked directly at me. He was no longer smiling.

"It's hard for people to understand in this Depression we're in, but back then, long before you were born, people were making money on all kinds of inventions and schemes. But only one pancake-making machine ever got made. And you're looking at it."

He turned his gaze back to the machine.

"Think of it. All those hours, days, and weeks he must have spent designing that thing, figuring out exactly how fast that shelf should move, figuring out how to control how much batter should come out. Think of all the motors, switches, and things he needed. And to what end? My mother lost her money. So did all those other people. Do you understand what I'm saying?"

"No," I said.

"Well, never mind. This is a strange world we live in Bobby. An awful lot of people struggle mightily and find it very hard to make it from one day to the next. These are hard times," he said as he continued to stare at the machine. "There really is nothing you can count on in this world of ours."

I was only in the first grade at PS 81. But I knew in the recesses of my mind that there was something called the Great Depression going on. There was evidence of it everywhere. We had passed a man selling pencils in the stairwell of the subway on our way to this restaurant. I knew that in some way such men were victims of the Depression.

But in my world I felt very secure. Very safe. My mother often told me that I should. I looked at her now. She was looking at my father. Her smile had disappeared. Her lips were pressed together. She turned to me. Her eyes widened and bore into me. Her head shook slowly from one side to the other as if to say, "Don't you believe it."

My mother rested in her Christian Science sense of God's perfection while my father was constantly trying to invent ways of improving the imperfections he saw.

JIMMY

Four years later, on another Sunday, I and five of my playmates sat in a row on the edge of my front porch with our feet on the step below, our elbows resting on our knees. It was raining. The overhang from the roof barely kept our feet dry. We all lived within one block of each other—Stephen, Francis, Buddy, his little brother Billy, and our ring leader, Jimmy. We all were ten except Billy who was eight. My friends had been to their Catholic church that morning while I attended the Christian Science church with my mother. My father had stayed home as usual.

"So whadaya wanna do?" Jimmy asked.

"I dunno," Buddy said. "Whadaya think we should do?"

We looked at Jimmy

"How about Communion?" Jimmy suggested. "I'll be the priest."

I began to feel a slight twinge of nervousness in my chest. I didn't like it when my friends talked about their church. They always said they were afraid of nuns and priests, and they always assumed that I shared their Catholic experiences. I didn't know what nuns or priests were; nor what they did. Jimmy often picked on me, and I was pretty sure it was because I wasn't Catholic. I didn't like feeling different because of my religion.

"We don't have any wine or wafers," Buddy said.

"We can pretend we have wine, and I can get some cookies from my mom for the body of Christ. I'll get a cup for the chalice. Bobby's porch can be the church."

What were they talking about? I was familiar with Christ. We called him Jesus or Christ Jesus. But I had no idea what eating cookies had to do with him.

Jimmy ran to his house and soon returned with a box of cookies and a cup. He told us to kneel in a line across the porch with our backs to his house. He stood over us with his back to my front door. I looked at the others and saw that they put their hands in front of them in an attitude of prayer. I copied them.

"Okay. Stick out your tongues," Jimmy ordered. Jimmy placed a cookie on each of our tongues and said "the body of Christ" each time.

Suddenly the front door opened, and my mother stepped out.

"What's going on?" she asked.

Jimmy spun around.

"We're playing Communion." he explained.

"You're playing Communion?" she asked as her brow furrowed and she sort of squinted. Her eyes fell on me. I still was kneeling with the cookie drying out on my tongue. "What are you doing with those cookies?" she asked.

"They're the body of Christ," Jimmy said.

Suddenly, I saw her wrinkled brow smooth out and her eyes widen. "Oh, for heaven's sake," she declared. "You mean like in your church? Well, I think you had better find something else to play. And stop staring at me with your tongues stuck out. You look ridiculous. You'd better get up and eat those cookies. Then you boys go and find something else to play. But before you go, Bobby, I want to talk to you." My friends disappeared off our porch. I followed my mother into the living room.

"Did you see that, James? They were reenacting a Catholic Communion service right on our front porch? You have to wonder if their nuns put them up to it—trying to convert Bobby."

Dad looked up from his paper. "I don't know, Katherine. How can you be so sure they were trying to convert Bobby?" He turned to me. "How did your game come about?"

"I dunno. We just decided to play."

"Now, Bobby," my mother said, "we both know *you* didn't decide to play Communion. What, after all, is Catholic Communion?"

"It's some kind of game they play in their church with cookies and wine. It's got something to do with a priest sticking a cookie on your tongue and saying 'Christ's body.'"

"You see, James! I just know those nuns put them up to it."

"Well," Dad said, "I find it hard to believe that the local nuns or priest could be bothered with one little boy."

"It's not only one little boy. It's Christian Science. I don't care what you say."

"You know, I've often heard you Christian Scientists expostulate on the Roman Catholic menace and how they hate Christian Science. To some extent, I understand. The Catholics would have us believe we are all damned to hell. And that is insulting. Be that as it may, I believe you do tend to overdo this Roman Catholic business."

My mother had complained a lot about the "oppressive atmosphere" she said the Catholics brought to our neighborhood. Everyone but us was Catholic. Nuns came onto our porch from time to time wanting to convert us.

"Honestly, James," she said. "I don't understand how you can be so complaisant. And I must say, Bobby, I can't imagine why you would have gone along with such a thing."

"But they're my friends. And besides, Jimmy's always picking on me. He always makes me be It when we play tag or hide-and-seek. Or he yells at me that I'm stupid."

Dad said, "So you're saying that you were afraid not to play Communion?"

"Well, yeah, sort of."

"Well now, that's another story." He paused. "You know, Bobby, there comes a time when you simply must stand up for yourself. I'll tell you what. You could use some boxing lessons. That should give you some confidence. We'll sign you up next week. Meantime, why don't you go on out and join your friends." He looked out the window. "Look, the sun's shining. I doubt they're still playing that church business."

◆   ◆   ◆

The next night, Mom and I ate dinner without Dad because he had to work late.

While we were eating she asked, "Didn't it bother you yesterday? Kneeling down like that and pretending Jimmy was a priest?"

"Sort of. I mean, we don't have anything like that in our church. Do we?"

"No. We don't. But we do practice communion."

"Do you eat cookies?"

"No, dear," she said as she chuckled a bit. "We do not eat cookies or drink wine or practice any kind of ritual other than kneeling silently in our own pew—all of us together. The word "communion" comes from the word "commune." So, what we do is silently kneel and commune with God. We let God's presence be in us, and we open ourselves to him. Then we recite the Lord's Prayer together. That's all."

"So, what do cookies have to do with it?"

"They have nothing to do with it. We use no symbols in the Christian Science church. But I want to get back to yesterday. First of all, I don't want you to think that I was complaining about your friends or their parents. They are not what I am concerned about. Can you understand that?"

"Sort of."

"Well, let me see if I can be clearer about this. Just a few days ago, I went over to Mrs. Farrell's to borrow a cup of sugar. You know that she is a devout Catholic."

"Yes."

"You also know she's quite deaf. So I had to walk right into her kitchen to get her attention. I found her there on her knees praying. I was about to turn around when she looked up and saw me. 'Oh, Mrs. Ellis,' she said, 'please help me. I know you pray differently from the way we do. But Bud is over there on Iwo Jima, and I'm so frightened.' She had her hands clasped in front of her holding her rosary beads.

"'We may pray differently, but we do pray to the same God,' I said. And I got down on my knees next to her. I closed my eyes, and we silently prayed together. I completely forgot about the sugar. It was so still in that room. I kept knowing silently that God was with us right there, and he was with Bud on Iwo Jima. I just knew it. I could feel God's presence. He was with us, caring for us, right in that room. And I knew Bud had to be feeling his presence too—all the way across the Pacific Ocean on that Japanese island.

"Then it was as though I heard a voice right next to me. It said, 'Don't you worry about Bud. He knows about me. He'll be all right.'

"I was so startled that I opened my eyes and looked over at Mrs. Farrell, but her eyes still were closed. I put my arm around her shoulder and gave her a little hug. She opened her eyes and looked at me with a gentle smile on her face. I could see that she wasn't so frightened anymore. So I got up and left. We didn't say a word.

"Mrs. Farrell is one of the dearest women I know, and I also know that Bud will be all right. He will come back. I just know we won't be seeing any gold star hanging in her window."

Gold stars hung in several of the windows in our neighborhood. They meant that the people living in those homes had a son who would not be coming back from the war. I hadn't known any of those people. But as I walked to school each day, it was very sad to see a gold star hanging in a window where I knew I hadn't seen one before.

"So you see," my mother continued, "it's not Mrs. Farrell. It's not any of our neighbors that I'm concerned about. No. It's what the Roman Catholic Church teaches. Their priests and nuns tell their parishioners that theirs is the only church. They teach their parishioners that all Protestants, and especially Christian Scientists, are damned to hell. The Roman Catholic Church has priests and nuns who dedicate their time to denying the efficacy of Christian Science. I know that seems hard to believe, but it is absolutely true.

"It all comes under the heading of animal magnetism," she said as she reached for her *Science and Health*. "Here's what Mrs. Eddy says: 'Animal magnetism … is the specific term for error or mortal mind.' Further on she says, 'there is no mortal mind, and consequently—'" here Mother emphasized the words, "'*no transference of mortal thought and willpower.*'"[1]

"What does that mean?" I asked.

"It means that it's not only a question of what people say about us. It's also a question of what people *think* about us. That's the heart of this subject. The whole point is not to allow other people's *thoughts* to ill effect us. We have to deny mental malpractice; that's what it's called. We must remember that there's only one Mind, and that Mind is God. No amount of thinking by other people can hurt us if we refuse to let it. And we must specifically deny that RC can have any effect on us because of the concerted effort by the priests directed at Christian Science."[2]

"RC?"

"That's what we call Roman Catholicism. We try not to dignify it with a name."

"Oh."

Yesterday my father had remarked that he thought Christian Scientists tended to overdo their objection to Roman Catholicism. I was confused on the subject. Except for Jimmy, my friends never bothered me. We just played. Yes, I felt different. But that was because I *was* different. I wasn't Catholic like them.

---

1. *Science and Health With Key to the Scriptures* by Mary Baker Eddy (*S&H*) 103:18 and following.
2. It's important to remember that this conversation took place in 1944. The "ecumenical movement" had never been heard of. Attitudes were very different then both in the Roman Catholic Church and in the Christian Science Church.

CONFIDENCE

My father signed me up for boxing lessons at the Neighborhood House, which was a community center next to PS 81, where I went to school. That next Thursday afternoon I stood outside with my hands dangling at my sides, weighted down with huge boxing gloves. Two other kids, Larry and John, stood beside me. We were all about the same height and age.

Mr. Foster, the instructor, looked us over. "All right boys," he said, "the first thing I want you to learn today is how to block a punch." He had us raise our arms and fists so that our hands were in front of our faces, and our elbows were extended down in front of our chest. Then he told me to see if I could prevent Larry from striking me. Suddenly, Larry's fist shot out, went right between my gloved hands and struck me hard on the nose. I fell backward and landed solidly on my seat.

"You okay, Bobby?" Mr. Foster asked as he helped me get up. I was stunned. My nose felt like mush. "Not so hard, Larry," Mr. Foster said. Larry looked just as surprised as I was. Mr. Foster explained, "Bobby, you should have moved your fists to block Larry's thrust. Now, John and Larry, let's see how you two do," Mr. Foster said.

John jabbed Larry in the face right away but not as hard. Then Larry hit John.

"Okay, boys. Now you understand how necessary it is to block your opponent's blows." He had us practice. Larry slowly threw a punch at my face, and Mr. Foster moved my hands so they stopped Larry's punch. We did it over and over until we were able to block fast punches. After a while, I began to feel I was getting the hang of it.

As the lesson concluded, Mr. Foster told us to practice our moves at home.

"I promise you," he said, "once you get it, you'll have a new sense of confidence."

Later at home, when nobody was looking, I tried throwing and blocking punches. At first I was awkward. But, with practice, I began to feel the sense of confidence Mr. Foster had promised.

◆   ◆   ◆

On the following Monday, I arrived home later than usual and found Jimmy and my other friends sitting on the steps leading up to my front porch.

"Hi, Bobby. Where you been? Teacher keep you after school?" Jimmy asked.

"No," I said as I tried to get by, but he got up and stood in my way.

"We've been missing you. Thought we could play hide-'n-seek, and you could be It. Wanna play?"

"Not now. I gotta go in. My mom's waiting for me."

"Oh his mommy's waiting for him," He looked at our friends. They stared back. He turned back to me. "Well, you're not going in until I say so."

Was he begging for a fight.

Suddenly, I lunged at him. He was really surprised, and he backed away. I flailed at him with punch after punch. I could see he didn't know anything about blocking. I was able to land several punches. It felt good. Finally, I was getting back at him.

Whack!

"That's for telling me I'm puny."

Thunk—right in his stomach.

"That's for the time you dropped my cat upside down off the porch roof."

Whack—to his chest.

"That's for blocking my stairs."

It went on and on. Back and forth we went. Fists flying. Our friends cheering.

We were on the long cement landing that our two houses shared. I kept my hands and arms in front of me and blocked a lot of his punches. Suddenly, an adult voice penetrated my hearing.

"What is going on out here?"

Jimmy and I stopped and stared at his front porch. Jimmy's mom stood there. "Are you two fighting?" We stood still panting really hard.

"No, Mom," Jimmy said.

"Well, it certainly looked to me as though you were. You come in here right this moment young man," she said to Jimmy. All the kids ran away. Jimmy turned around slowly and headed toward his porch.

"You should be ashamed of yourself young man," Jimmy's mom said to him.

I turned and went up the steps to our porch and into our apartment. My mom was in the kitchen at the back of the house. I guessed she hadn't heard anything.

"What happened to you? Look at you. Your shirt tails are hanging out. Your hair's a mess, and you're all red in the face! Have you been in a fight?"

"Jimmy and I kinda had a fight. We punched each other a few times."

"You had a fist fight with Jimmy?"

"Yeah. The kids were all sitting on the steps, and Jimmy wouldn't get out of my way. Dad told me to stand up to him. So I did."

Mom stared at me for a moment. I watched her eyes narrow. Then she said—almost to herself—"I don't know what to say." There was another pause. "Well I'm sorry it came to this. I certainly don't approve of your fighting."

◆   ◆   ◆

When Dad came home that night, Mom told him what had happened.

"I never expected you to get into it so soon," he said. "How did you do? Did you win?"

"Oh James! Really!"

"I don't know. Sort of I guess. I mean he didn't hurt me or anything."

"So do you think he got his comeuppance?" my father asked.

"I dunno. He came out after, and he said he was surprised the way I got him really good a couple of times. Then a bunch of us played tag. This time I didn't have to be It."

◆   ◆   ◆

The next morning, Dad left before I got up. While I was eating breakfast, my mother sat across the table from me.

"There's something I want to talk to you about. She paused briefly then said, "I'm not condemning what happened yesterday. I can understand that boys will get themselves into these situations. My concern is over how you meet the challenges you may be facing. What is the first thing you should do when you're confronted? Should you simply be ready to fight? Or is there something else?"

"Uh … I dunno."

"Well, let's see how I can explain," She thought for a minute. "You must be aware that I've been mentally working very hard to know that no suggestion of bullying can be allowed to touch you."

"Uh, yeah." I knew that no matter where my mother was or what she was doing, she was silently working to know that only God was directing her and me and Dad and everyone.

She continued, "If we allow the idea that we are subject to bullying to reside in our consciousness, then the likelihood is that we will experience bullying. Such claims are what Mrs. Eddy calls "aggressive mental suggestion." She instructs us to deny aggressive mental suggestion every day. So I have been denying to myself that bullying can be a part of your experience and knowing that only God is in control. Or, if bullying does seem to be directed at you, it cannot harm you."

"So your prayers helped me. I never thought I'd fight Jimmy, and maybe even beat him," I said.

"I must reiterate that I am not condoning fist fights. But I do believe you were beautifully protected in this instance," she paused, and then continued, "It's quite wonderful. When divine intelligence operates in our thinking, the most amazing solutions come about; like directing us to take human footsteps such as boxing lessons. So, on your way to school, remember that God is caring for you."

"Okay," I said. I kissed my mother on the cheek and headed out the kitchen door.

My mother often spoke to me in this manner. Her words were comforting even if what she said might, at times, have been over my head. Her words expressed an atmosphere of caring both on her part and on the part of God which was very assuring.

The very next day, another bully who loved to taunt me followed me down the path through the woods from our school. Other kids were following us as he yelled, "Where're you going, Bobby? Going home to Mommy? Afraid to fight?"

The other kids joined in. "Yeah, Bobby? You gonna fight Tony?"

In days past, I had hunched my head into my shoulders and hurried along as fast as I could. Always in the past, Tony had gotten tired of it and turned around. But this time, I turned and faced him. "You wanna fight? Okay, let's fight," I said as I dropped my books and lunch pail to the ground and I raised my fists.

"Oh. Wow!" the kids yelled.

Tony stared at me for a long time. Finally, he said, "Nah. That's okay." With that, he turned around and headed back toward the school, and the rest of the kids melted away.

I felt really good. I didn't know if it was Mom's prayers or Dad's lessons or both. Whatever it was, I had gained a sense of self-confidence I never had experienced before. I was never the victim of bullying again.

So maybe I could feel confident in my religion in spite of the fact that I was the only Christian Science kid in our area. On the other hand, I never would have stood up to Jimmy or Tony if it hadn't been for those boxing lessons. Which was it? Mom's faith? Dad's instruction? Or both?

NIGHTMARES

Several months later, I started having nightmares—the same nightmare every night. My parents would hear me screaming and waken me in a terrified state. One night after one of these bouts, I lay in my bed as Mom sat on the edge.

I said, "I'm really scared, Mom."

"I know. It has been awful," she said. She paused for a moment. "I do understand. Many children have scary dreams. But that doesn't mean that we have to accept them. I have an idea. Would you like to try a little mental exercise?"

"Okay. But how come when John is sick, Aunt Dorothy gives him a pill, and it makes him better? Why can't I have a pill to make me better?" I asked.

Earlier that year, my mother had to go to Columbus, Ohio, to see her mother and father for a week. So she left me with Aunt Dorothy and my cousins in Leonia, New Jersey. I got really sick. My aunt took me to a doctor who prescribed some pills for me. Aunt Dorothy said, "Bobby, I'll feel so much better if you do as the doctor is asking." So I took the pill, and then I took several more during the next few days.

"I doubt they have a pill for nightmares," my mother said. "But Aunt Dorothy and I talked about it after I got back from Columbus. She was concerned that I might be upset. I assured her that I was simply grateful to her for caring for you. You see, all we can ask of any individual is that she act according to her highest sense of right. I would never condemn anyone for doing what they believe to be the best for you.

"Now, let's do that little mental exercise I suggested. Can you repeat the seven synonyms for God?"

We were taught in Sunday school that there were seven words that meant the same as God. I repeated them: "Life. Truth. Principle. Mind. Spirit. Soul. Love."

"Excellent. As you know, each of these words equals God. Everything we need to know about God is expressed in these seven synonyms. They denote God both collectively and individually. But sometimes it's helpful to concentrate on one synonym in order to handle or deal with a particular problem. In this case, what would you say we need to handle?"

"Uh … I'm scared of the dream. Scared to go to sleep," I said.

"Yes. I would say fear is what we must handle. So how can we counteract that fear? What synonym of God will help us establish the fact that there is no room for fear in our consciousness?"

"Um, Mind?"

"And why Mind?"

"Because God is infinite, and if he's infinite, then only his Mind exists, and God isn't afraid of anything?"

"That's wonderful, Bobby. That's exactly right. But, you know, I was thinking of another synonym. Can you imagine what that would be?"

"Uh … I dunno."

"Well, I was thinking of Love. And for the same reasons you gave. If God is infinite, then he is infinite Love, and there is no room for fear. Divine Love could never experience fear. Thinking of Divine Love makes us realize that God cares and protects every one of his ideas. You are one of his ideas, so God cares for you. He loves you. Think of the way a robin spreads her wings over her chicks, loving and protecting them. Just like that robin, God is loving and protecting you right now.

"Let's do this. I'll leave now, and you try to know that God's love is filling this room. Let God enter your thoughts."

She got up from my bed, left the bedside light on, and closed the door half-way. I rolled over on my side and saw my *Science and Health* and the Bible on my bedside table. Suddenly, it was as if I heard a voice. "Pick up your *Science and Health*." I opened it randomly. My eyes focused on the words "God is Love." Mom had just finished talking about this synonym. I felt my eyes widen. Then I read the sentence, "The starting point of divine Science is that God, Spirit, is All-in-all, and that there is no other might nor Mind—that God is Love."[1] I settled back into my pillow and clutched the book to my chest with both hands. I closed my eyes and thought, "I'm only going to think of God, of Love. Nothing else. I won't let any other thoughts come into my head." I awoke the next morning with the book lying beside me.

When I went into the kitchen my mother asked, "How are you, dear? You seem to have had a good night's sleep."

"Yeah. I still was scared after you left. But then it was like someone told me to pick up *Science and Health*. I opened it, and I saw the words 'God is Love.' So I told myself not to let anything but Love come into my head. The next thing I knew, I woke up just now."

---

1.   *S&H* Page 275

"You know what this means, don't you?" she asked.

"No. What?"

"It means, dear, that you have just had your first healing where you worked things out for yourself. I'm so grateful, Bobby. I believe this is a milestone."

I never had any more nightmares.

There are no miracles in Christian Science. Rather, I was taught that Christian Scientists bring about healings in the same way Jesus did—by understanding that Jesus's "mighty works (were) not supernatural, but supremely natural"[2] according to the perfect law of God.

Now, all of a sudden, Christian Science healing seemed real to me in every day life.

---

2.   *S&H* xi:14

UNIFORMS

About a year later, I came home from school one day and handed an envelope to my mother. "Mrs. Simpson told us to give you this letter," I said. Mrs. Simpson was principal of our school. I was in the sixth grade.

My mother read the letter. "Hmmm … it seems that a lot of the boys come to school dressed sloppily, so Mrs. Simpson wants you all to wear shirts and ties from now on."

The next morning, Saturday, at breakfast, Mom handed Dad the letter. "You got home too late last night for me to show this to you, James."

He read the letter, then said, "I've never read such a thing. This is completely unacceptable! I will not have it!"

"What do you mean?" my mom asked.

"Certainly you can see that Mrs. Simpson is trying to turn PS 81 into a Catholic school like St. Mary's. Those kids wear uniforms, so she wants the public school kids to wear uniforms. It's outrageous. Public schools don't have uniforms. It's only that Catholic influence that's going on here. As much as I hate to admit it, you had some reason to be concerned over that Catholic business on our porch."

"Oh James, I don't know. Mrs. Simpson just wants the boys to come to school dressed neatly."

"Then let them dress neatly. But I'm here to tell you this is nothing more than a separation-of-church-and-state issue. Bobby has never gone to school dressed other than neatly, and he will continue to do so."

"But James, what's he to say to Mrs. Donahue?"

Mrs. Donahue was my teacher.

"He'll have to tell her we refused. He can stand up for his rights just like anybody else. It's time he learned to do so. This will be a good lesson for him."

"You're asking Bobby to stand up against the whole school?"

"It's not the whole school, Katherine. It's the attempt to turn a public school into a parochial school. There is not a single public school in the city of New York, I wager, or in the United States that requires its students to wear a uniform. That's strictly a church school requirement."

"The Fieldston kids wear uniforms, Daddy."

"Well, yes, Bobby; that's correct. But Fieldston is a private school. Those kids' parents pay tuition for their kids to attend there. And they agree in advance to the condition of their children wearing the school uniform. However, any child who does not attend a private or parochial school must attend a public school. They have no choice. Public schools are run by the state. And no church is allowed to have anything to do with the state. Separation of church and state is spelled out in the very First Amendment of the Bill of Rights. The Bill of Rights is what sets our country apart from all other nations. But I can understand why you might be reticent about this. So, what I'll do is write a letter for you to bring to Mrs. Donahue. I have to go to work now. But tomorrow, I'll make some phone calls and find out how some of the other parents feel."

After my father left Mom asked, "Are you all right?"

"I guess so. But why is Daddy doing this to me? I mean, I'll be the only kid in school without a tie on."

"Oh, Bobby. Daddy's not doing this to you. It's just that, perhaps for the first time, you've been caught up in his beliefs. Your father is one of the most highly moral men I have ever known. He insists on doing what is right, no matter what. And in this case, he's including you in his concept of what's morally correct."

"But how does he know it's right for me not to wear a tie?"

"That is a difficult question. How does anyone know what is right in any situation? And that comes down to where we turn for our answers. While we turn to God for our answers, Daddy looks for his sense of right and wrong by looking toward his highest sense of human good. Do you see the difference?"

"I guess so," I replied, but I wasn't at all certain that I understood.

"Well, what do we learn in church or Sunday school about how to know what to do when we're confronted with a problem?"

"We ask God for things, like 'How can I get Dad to let me wear a tie to school?'"

"It's true that most people think of praying as being a way of asking God *for* something. That type of prayer is what's called a prayer of petition.

"But in Christian Science, we use a prayer of acknowledgment. We acknowledge God's presence. We even express gratitude to God for being with us right here and now even though we don't have our answers. We acknowledge that the answer will come to us from God. As an example, it may be that Daddy is correct in his not wanting you to wear that tie to school. And you have to trust that if that is the case, then God will direct you and me and Daddy in exactly what we should do, day by day, hour by hour."

My mother was telling me that my father listened to God even if he didn't know it. It was confusing. How did he know that his answers were the right ones if he wasn't a Christian Scientist? She often explained my father's ways to me in the light of her own understanding. But I always knew my father was not a Christian Scientist. Once, when I asked him if he believed in God, he told me that he was an agnostic.

"It means that I don't know if there is a God or not," he said.

I would learn as the years went by that he hated Christian Science even though, in my presence, he stayed silent on the subject for many years.

◆   ◆   ◆

That next Monday morning, I went to school wearing one of my regular sport shirts and no tie. I kept my shoulders hunched forward and my chin as low as I could, hoping no one would notice that I wasn't wearing a tie.

Mrs. Donahue asked each of the boys to give her Mrs. Simpson's letters, which our parents were supposed to have signed. She looked over the whole class, and then her eyes settled on me.

"Bobby, you were supposed to wear a dress shirt and tie today."

"My father told me not to wear a tie. He said it was a violation of the separation of church and state. He told me to say that."

Except for me and Mrs. Donahue, there was no sound in the classroom. All eyes were on me. I wanted to slide under my desk.

"Separation of church and state? What does he mean?"

"I don't know."

She looked at all the other boys. Then she noticed Herbie Goldman and Ben Williams.

"Herbie? Ben? Why do you not have dress shirts and ties on?" she asked.

"My parents said the same thing—violation of church and state," Herbie answered.

"Ben?"

"Yes, Mrs. Donahue. My parents did too. My parents said they agree with Mr. Ellis," Ben said.

"Ah. So your parents conferred over this? Well, children, I will have to talk with Mrs. Simpson during recess."

◆   ◆   ◆

Just before three o'clock, Mrs. Donahue told me, Ben, and Herbie to stay seated. The three o'clock bell rang, and everybody else rushed out of class. Mrs. Donahue said, "Mrs. Simpson is very concerned, but she understands that it is your parents with whom we must talk. So, I have a letter for each of you to take home to your parents," she said as she handed each of us an envelope. "I'll want a response tomorrow morning."

◆   ◆   ◆

My mother read the letter as soon as I handed it to her. "Mrs. Simpson says she wants to meet with the parents on Wednesday morning," she said as she finished reading.

When my father got home, my mother showed him the letter.

"Hmm. A meeting, eh? Well, yes that's a good idea."

"So how did it go with you?" Dad asked me.

"Okay, I guess."

"So you see, Bobby. You stood up for your rights, and it was okay."

"I guess so. So, now can I wear a tie?" I still had no idea what rights I had protected. I only wanted to be the same as the rest of my classmates.

"No, no Bobby. We must stand up for our rights in this situation, and we are correct in taking this stand. I'd better call the Williamses and the Goldmans and make sure we're all together on this."

◆   ◆   ◆

When I got home on Wednesday, I asked my mother what had happened at the meeting.

"Well it was very interesting. There were quite a few parents in Mrs. Simpson's office, and they didn't like Mrs. Simpson's edict. Mrs. Simpson was quite adamant about her demands for a shirt and tie. But Daddy was firm in his position. He agreed with Mrs. Simpson that children going to school should be dressed properly. But he objected to any uniform. She said she would take the matter under advisement."

◆   ◆   ◆

About a week later, I came home with another letter. My mother read it: "Hmm. Mrs. Simpson's no longer insisting on a dress shirt and tie. She says that her point has been made. She is satisfied that the boys are now coming to school dressed neatly," she said as she looked at me. "So, you see? Daddy was right. And we were right in trusting that God would take care."

So it would seem that both Mom's prayers and Dad's high sense of right worked. But the difference in my parents' understanding of how to know what was right was confusing.

SIGNS

"Have you noticed, Bobby, that most of the houses on our street don't have any numbers on them? Not even our house? I think there's an opportunity for you here. You could sell all those people a number sign for their house," my dad said one early spring morning as we ate our breakfast at the kitchen table. I now was in the seventh grade.

I had no idea what suddenly caused my father to make this suggestion. All I could think to say was, "But, Dad, where would I get numbered signs?"

"You can make them. You have your workbench and all the tools you need. You'll just have to get some supplies—wood, numbers, uh … let's see … creosote. You'll produce a high quality product that will last. You'll put the signs on stakes, which can go into peoples' front lawns, and you'll be able to show that they won't rot because you've creosoted the part that goes into the ground. This'll give you some excellent experience in designing, manufacturing, and selling a product, and you'll make some money to boot."

Monday morning after he left for work and before I left for school, I asked my mother, "Why does Dad want me to sell signs?"

"Perhaps he wants you to have some door-to-door experience. He goes door-to-door through all the office buildings downtown and drums up business. He's good at it."

That Tuesday, Dad didn't have to leave for work early so he drove me to school. "I've been thinking about your sign project. This afternoon, after school, why don't you go to Johnson's Hardware over on Broadway and find out what different sizes of lumber are available. I think you'll need something about four inches wide and one-half-inch thick for the signs. And the stakes could be something like one-and-a-half inches square. And see what they have in the way of numbers. Then we can set about designing your signs, figuring out how to manufacture them, and deciding how much you'll need to charge."

Friday night he came home in time for us to have dinner together. "Here's a design I've drawn for your sign. I think it will be very well received by your customers," he said as he reached into his shirt pocket and handed me a sketch of a sign with our house number—6223—on it. It showed a stake in the ground holding a sign with jagged ends that resembled pointed teeth carved out of the wood. "I figure a nice rustic look would be good."

"But, Dad, how do we make something like this?"

"You'll set up a production line so you can mass produce them."

"Mass produce?"

"Yes. You'll precut several signs and stakes at one time. The stakes can be soaking in creosote until you need them. We'll set up a jig so you can cut the jagged ends of the signs, and you'll whittle the points to make them look hand-carved. You'll also need a jig for cutting points in the stakes so they can be easily driven into the ground. Once you've taken an order, you can remove a stake from the creosote, dry it, and stain it. Meantime, you can stain your signs in advance so they can be dry and ready for fastening to the stake. Then you can apply the numbers and deliver the finished product to your customer. So let's see what you have," he said, He was enthusiastically rubbing his hands together as he got up from the table.

I showed him what the lumber man had given me and a sample number. "All right. This is good information. So, here's what I want you to do. Tomorrow, go back to Johnson's and buy a short piece of sign lumber, maybe four feet or so, and do the same for the stake material. You'll also want to find out how the stain comes—quarts or gallons—and how much it costs. Also, get a color chart from them so we can pick out a good color. Then on Sunday, you can try making a sign. This will just be a prototype."

"A prototype?"

"Yes. It'll be a test to see how you go about making something that actually will look all right and something you can sell and produce easily. You might have to try more than once before you get it right. This is going to be great fun. You'll see. Here's five dollars for the supplies. It shouldn't come to anything like that. All we need for now is the lumber. So bring me back the change."

"Okay," was all I could say.

Saturday morning, I came home from Johnson's with two short pieces of left-over lumber for the signs and the stakes, as well as the color chart. I put the stuff on top of my littered workbench in my bedroom, and I set Dad's change on top of the pile.

As soon as he got home Saturday night he said, "Let's take a look."

I followed him into my room. He counted the change and put it in his pants pocket. Then he examined the lumber.

"This is very good. It'll be very easy to work with. It's pine, but it doesn't have a lot of knots in it, so it should be quite easy to carve the ends. Well, let's go have dinner. Then we can come back to your workbench and start figuring out exactly how to make your signs."

◆   ◆   ◆

Two weeks later, I approached the front door of my first potential customer with my prototype number sign in hand. The lady who responded to my very timid knock ordered a sign. The cost was $2.89. Dad told me that people will buy things if there's a 9 in the price. The lady thought the price was very reasonable, and the sign would look very well on her lawn.

I knew several kids in our primarily Irish Catholic neighborhood. But many of the households were childless. I didn't know those people, but they all were very nice to me as I went from door-to-door. I sold lots of signs. They showed up on front lawns all over our immediate neighborhood and even in Yonkers. I became amazingly bold as I went from door-to-door selling house numbers.

I returned home with the weekend's four or five orders. I pulled the needed stakes from the creosote, stained their tops, and set them out to dry. Then I applied the appropriate numbers to the signs I had already made. The next day, the stakes were dry. I fastened them to the signs with screws, which went in through drilled holes at the top of the stakes and into the signs just deep enough to hold them but not so deep as to penetrate the front.

During the week, after school, I cut more stakes and signs, set the stakes to soaking in creasote, stained the signs, and left them to dry. The next weekend, I would deliver the previous weekend's orders as I walked around the neighborhood and called on more households. Most people didn't want my signs. But enough people ordered them to make the venture seem worthwhile enough to satisfy my father.

Early on, however, we discovered one difficulty. Not everyone wanted a sign stuck in their lawn. Some people wanted the sign fastened to their house or perhaps a porch post.

"What do you think?" Dad asked. "How will you handle that?"

"Well, I was thinking that instead of attaching the sign to the stake, we could fasten a block of wood to the back of the sign. It'd only be as long as the width of the sign so it wouldn't show. But before we fasten the block to the sign, we could put two nails through it. The nails would stick out the back so you could pound the sign into the house."

"Excellent. Of course, you'll have to use a block of wood on the sign to protect it from your hammer when you pound it into their post, but it ought to work."

From then on, I carried two prototypes with me.

But selling and making signs took time, and I had other important things to do, like playing with my friends. At first they thought I was nuts. Then they thought my signs were neat as they began to appear on various lawns. But soon, the novelty wore off. Even Dad stopped checking with me on my success. It seemed the point had been made.

As the years went by, I spent many hours following my father around, helping him rig various contraptions, and performing repairs on our home. Dad never interfered with my mother's religious instruction, but he gave me many lessons in the practicalities of his world compared to my mother's spiritual approach.

ELECTRIC CHAIR

One Sunday evening during the early fall when I was thirteen and in the eighth grade, my family was sitting in the living room listening to the Ralph Edwards radio show *Truth or Consequences*. If contestants gave the correct answer to a question, bells and whistles went off, and they received a prize. With a wrong answer, a raucous buzzer blasted, and the contestant suffered a consequence. Tonight's contestant didn't know that a wrong answer would get her a hot seat.

Mr. Edwards asked the question. The contestant gave a wrong answer. The buzzer went off, and the contestant just sat there. The buzzer bleated again. Nothing! It sounded a third time. Still nothing! Finally, Mr. Edwards told the contestant that an electric shock should have made her jump out of the chair.

"Oh? Perhaps the shock couldn't get through my rubber girdle," She replied.

The audience laughed uproariously. We still had tears in our eyes when I said, "I wonder how they make a hot seat?"

Dad wiped his eyes and said, "Well, I imagine they have wires in the seat that transmit a current into the people when they push the buzzer. It wouldn't be difficult to make. In fact, we could turn your chair into a hot seat. All you would have to do is take some lamp wire, strip all the insulation off, unravel it so that you have the individual strands, thread a needle with one of the strands, and weave it in and out of the fabric."

"Now you two just stop this right now!" Mom said. "Let's have it understood that I'll not have such goings on in my living room with my wing-back chair."

Dad smiled a tiny bit and then looked back at me. "Of course, simple house current could electrocute someone. You'd want to have mostly voltage going through; you wouldn't want many amps. Amps do the damage. So what we would need to do is *convert* the amps into volts with an induction coil—like the one in our car? I'm pretty sure I have one at the factory. I'll tell you what. I'll look for it tomorrow and bring it home."

◆   ◆   ◆

Monday night, just in time for dinner, Dad came home and handed me a paper bag as I kissed him hello on his cheek. I reached into the bag and pulled out the coil. We went straight to my room.

"Let's see how we can do this," Dad said. "Do you have your six-volt battery?"

"Right here," I said as I picked the battery up off the workbench.

"Okay then," Dad said, "let's see if we can make this work." He put a piece of metal that was sticking out of the coil into the vise.

"What's that?" I asked.

"That's the mounting plate. It's where it normally would be fastened to the car. It also is the ground. As you can see, there's only one wire coming out of the top. So the circuit is completed through the car itself and back into the coil via this plate. So your vise can be the car. We'll hook up those two wires on the bottom to your battery. Then, if we hold the end of the top wire close to the vise, we should see a spark."

"What are you two doing?" Mom asked from the doorway to my room. "Dinner has been ready since you came home, James, and it's not getting any better."

"We'll be right there, Katherine," Dad said. "We've just about finished."

Neither of us looked up. This was man stuff. Mom couldn't possibly understand.

"Okay. Let's try it," Dad said. "Here, take hold of the cable and bring the copper strands almost to the vise. Be sure you touch only the insulation. If we have this right, there'll be a pretty good spark, and it will go to the closest ground it can find. That could be you! We wouldn't want you to get electrocuted, would we?" he said as he chuckled a bit.

I very carefully followed Dad's instructions and nearly jumped to the ceiling as a spark flew from the wire to the vise over at least a quarter-inch gap.

◆   ◆   ◆

Two weeks later we were ready. Somehow we had gotten Mom to let us use her black-and-gold wingback chair. She even helped me weave the strands into the seat. A length of the copper strand was left free so it could be run down behind the chair's leg and kept out of sight. From there, the strand was run from the Oriental rug next to the chair to a wire, which ran under the rug and across the room to the area behind a waste basket where we had hidden the coil and battery. To complete the circuit another strand went up the opposite front leg of the chair and into the chair's fabric in the same way.

Dad volunteered to be our first victim. He sat in the chair. We had one of the two wires to the battery fully attached. I was to touch the other wire to the battery to administer the shock.

"Go ahead," he said, though he looked rather tense as he sat in the chair.

I briefly touched the wire to the battery.

Dad didn't move. He had me hold the wire directly on the battery, "Hmm, well, I'm not feeling anything. Let me try something."

He put his hands on the wires in the seat.

"Wow!" he yelped. "There's juice there, all right. Our clothes must be acting as insulation—like that lady's rubber girdle. That's not very helpful, is it? We hardly can expect people to sit on their hands or in the nude, can we?" He laughed. "I guess we're going to have to put the wires into each arm of the chair so that when people sit down, their hands will rest on the wires."

I spent the next week of after-school hours unraveling the wires from the seat of Mom's wing-back chair and weaving them into the arms. By the next weekend, we were ready. And this time, I had a victim. He was my best friend, Ben Williams. I had spent the week in school telling him that I was working on a new science project at home.

He came over Sunday afternoon after church. He, my father and I headed into the living room. "Okay. Here's how it works," I said to Ben. "You sit in that chair."

The chair sat on the polished hardwood floor with its front legs just touching the Oriental rug. He sat down. "Now I'm going to hypnotize you without saying anything. I'm just going to look at you, and when you're really relaxed, you'll do something I want you to do even though I don't actually tell you to do it."

Ben leaned back and put his forearms on the arms of the chair with his hands exactly where they needed to be. He really relaxed—he even almost closed his eyes. Slowly, I let my right hand drop to my side. I found the wire without looking away from Ben, and I touched it to the battery pole.

His hands flew off the arms of the chair, but he didn't realize what had happened. He put his hands back on the arms and pressed down hard to push himself up and out of the chair. He got a tremendous charge and leaped out of the chair really hard. The chair flew back over the wood floor, knocked over a floor lamp, and crashed into a bookcase. Knickknacks and books tumbled to the floor.

"What on earth is going on in here?" Mom asked as she came rushing into the living room. Dad and I stood in silent awe.

"What happened?" was all Ben could say as he looked toward Mom.

"We just electrocuted you!"

"Now look at what you two have done!" Mom exclaimed. "How could you do such a thing? And to your best friend. You two clean up that mess."

"But what happened?" Ben asked.

Dad and I started picking up the room. "We made a hot seat, and you were our first guinea pig," I said as I showed him how I had rigged the chair. "The only problem is that you have to give the shock through the arms of the chair since the voltage from the induction coil isn't high enough to go through your clothes."

"You know, Bobby, I've been thinking about that," Dad said. "What you need is a Model-T Ford induction coil. They produce twenty thousand volts. That really would zap someone. I imagine you could buy one from O'Henry's over on Broadway." He paused and then said, "You know what you could do, Bobby. You could make a cushion with wires in it. You could put something like that on any chair anywhere you wanted."

"What's a Model T Ford?"

"They were cars that the Ford Company made before you were born."

"Now look here," Mom said. "Enough is enough. I've gone along with as much as I'm going to. I'm putting my foot down. It's not going any further in this house." She stalked into the kitchen and rattled lots of pots and pans. But I knew that my mom wouldn't really stop me from pursuing this really neat experiment with my dad.

◆   ◆   ◆

It took a week and a half for Mr. O'Henry to get me the Model T Ford induction coil. Meanwhile, I spent the time unraveling the wires from Mom's chair and making an electric cushion. It was about an inch thick, one foot long, and eight or nine inches wide. Mom helped me sew a cover for it so that the wires didn't show at all.

Ben was with me when I brought the coil home. We stood in my room staring at it for a long time. It was rectangular, with a wood casing. It stood about four inches high, six inches long, and two inches wide. Two quarter-inch bolts extended from the top. They were about four inches apart. On one end were two smaller terminals clearly intended to be attached to the battery. Finally, I said, "Let's hook up the battery. Then we can take a screwdriver and hold the metal rod on one of those poles; then we'll slowly slide it over toward the other pole until we get something."

I attached the battery's wires to the two smaller terminals. A hum came from the box. I picked up the screwdriver, touched its tip to one of the poles on the coil, and slowly moved it toward the other pole.

The next thing I knew, I was sitting in the middle of my bedroom floor. Somehow, I had touched the metal on the screwdriver and the other pole. I went flying. Lionel train cars and tools flew all over the place.

"What happened?" Mom yelled as she came into my room.

I was on the floor with my eyes bugging out. Ben was sitting on the bed with his eyes bugging out, and the room was a shambles.

"Are you two all right? What did you do?" she asked.

"I got a little shock. We got Dad's Model T Ford induction coil. That's it." I pointed at my workbench. Somehow the coil had not moved. It still was humming. "Want to see? It's really neat."

"Well, all right," Mom said.

I got up from the floor, put a few things back, and found the screwdriver. I could see that the metal shank in the screwdriver continued through the wood handle to a metal button on the end of the handle. I must have touched that button, making *me* the ground Dad had described. This time, I was able to hold the screwdriver in place without touching the metal button. I got a really neat blue spark about one and one-half inches long. It crackled really loud and it made a funny, fresh-air smell. Dad told me later that the smell was ozone.

"I have to admit, that is quite something," Mom said. "Well, all right boys. I'm glad you're okay. Let's get this mess cleaned up."

Ben and I carefully disconnected the battery from the coil and picked up most of what had gone flying when I got my jolt. While cleaning up, we began figuring out how we could trick more victims. I had shown Ben the wired cushion. We decided to start a secret hypnosis club. Anybody wanting to join our club would have to let us hypnotize him and then promise not to tell what we had done. We ended up hypnotizing almost every kid in our eighth grade class. It was neat the way they would wiggle like crazy and then jump out of the chair.

Soon however, everybody knew what we had. Finally, I brought my hot seat contraption into science class. I explained how the induction coil worked, and I showed how, with all that voltage in the air, if you put your head near the coil your hairs would stand up. If you brought a florescent tube near the coil, the tube would light up without any wires.

I lost count of how many times I got a twenty-thousand-volt jolt from that coil. I even touched the poles by mistake in front of our science class. Everybody laughed.

"Are you all right, Bobby?" Mrs. Fischer asked.

I assured her I was.

"Where did you learn so much about electricity?" she asked.

"From my father."

She said, "Well, I must say this was quite instructive."

Two years earlier, after one of my first science classes with Mrs. Fischer, I had declared some new knowledge to my father when I exclaimed, "That's steam," while pointing to a pot of water, which was boiling on our stove. "Mrs. Fischer showed us that today."

"Oh, no it's not," Dad had responded. "That's water vapor. Steam is invisible. If you could look at the very surface of the water, you'd see that there's a little space between the water and the vapor. The steam condenses into the vapor when it hits the cooler air. Mrs. Fischer should know better."

The next day, I corrected Mrs. Fischer. She did not agree with my father until I told her that my father had shown me in the dictionary that he was correct. She was not pleased. I wondered if she'd ever forgive me and my father for showing her up in class, although that had not been my intention. I had thought she would be pleased with my bringing her the correct information.

Today, it seemed all was forgiven. Dad's formal education had never advanced beyond high school, but he sure did know a lot. I felt quite proud of him as I picked up my induction coil, wires, and cushion and returned to my seat near the back of the classroom. Figuring things out with him was a lot of fun.

MCBURNEY

I was set to graduate from PS 81 in June of 1948. That was just around the corner, so my parents and I had been trying to figure out where I should attend high school. Today we were being given a tour of McBurney School for Boys on W. Sixty-fifth Street just off Central Park West in Manhattan.

But, there was no way I would be able to get in. It was so humiliating. I took entrance exams for the Bronx School of Science and for the Fieldston School in Riverdale, and I had flunked. There was a lot of math on the test that had not been covered at PS 81.

And private schools meant you had to pay to attend, so it didn't seem very likely. We always had food on the table, but Mom had a problem getting money out of Dad for the rent or for the coal. How were they ever going to afford three hundred dollars a semester for this school? That's what it cost. Dad told me. Mom never let me know about these things. She didn't want me to "worry unnecessarily." But Dad didn't want me to get my hopes too high. No. I was destined to go to DeWitt Clinton High School in the middle of the Bronx where there were thousands of kids with ducktail haircuts and switchblade knives.

Still, we were at McBurney because Dad had suggested it. He came home one night and told Mom about a new customer of his who was an education counselor. He had told the counselor about our search for the right school. She had quizzed him about me and my failed efforts at getting into some school other than DeWitt Clinton. She suggested he look at McBurney. I couldn't help but wonder why he would have talked with that woman and then brought us here if there wasn't some chance of my attending. And my mother had assured me I could trust that God would show us where I belonged.

"I know you are facing what seems a difficult future for your schooling. But we have to trust that next fall you will be exactly where you belong. We have to let God direct us to where you belong—not my intelligence, not Daddy's, not yours. We need to get our own will out of the way."

"Well," the guide said, "we better move on. Let me show you the gym." He had already shown us a swimming pool, a library, a chemistry lab, and a physics lab. Now we walked into the gym. There were parallel bars, trampolines, and ropes hanging from the ceiling. A track was suspended up high around the edge of the room.

"Being a YMCA school," he said, "we have a regular calisthenics program. All the boys must participate. Also, there are various teams that you can try out for. Gymnastics, swimming, football, baseball, soccer, track, tennis. Or you might want to go into other activities. We have a wonderful extracurricular drama program here too. Let me show you our theater."

He brought us into a real theater. With a real stage and curtains and lights and scenery.

I had never seen anything like this school before. Was there any chance I might be able to go here?

As he explained more about the school, our guide led us back to the entrance. He shook hands with Mom and Dad. Then he turned and shook my hand. "Well, Bobby, I hope you enjoyed our tour. We'd love to have you attend school here come next fall!" he said as he turned to my parents. "We'll be sending you a letter of acceptance in a few days."

I was dumbstruck. They wanted me to attend? Mom was smiling broadly. Dad had a bit of a smile too. Was it possible? Was this where I belonged? I was floating on air as we left the school and walked to the Fifty-ninth Street IRT subway entrance. As our train approached the 157th Street Station on Broadway, Dad turned to us and said, "Well, I'll see you two later." And he got off the train. He had left work to take the tour of McBurney.

The doors closed, and the train continued. I stayed lost in my thoughts. At Dykeman Street, the train emerged from below ground. Sunlight poured in, and I blurted out, "It really works, Mom. Doesn't it?"

"What's that, dear?"

"Knowing you'll be where you belong. Knowing God is taking care of you."

"Yes, dear. It does work."

"But it's so hard, Mom."

"I know. It can seem very difficult to understand and trust. But that's what we have to do. And when we do, God always is there taking care of us. Just look at where we are today."

At the end of the line we got off the train and got on the bus. As I watched Van Courtland Park go by our window, it dawned on me. "I think I get it, Mom. Because we trusted God, he caused Dad to meet that education lady who suggested McBurney. And that's how we ended up visiting McBurney. And now they want me to go there."

My mother nodded. I knew that money would be a big obstacle. Dad had been quiet during most of our tour. Unlike Mom's, his message had always been, "Sure you take the good with the bad. But you can be certain the bad will be ever present."

◆   ◆   ◆

Soon after I graduated from PS 81 we moved from Spencer Avenue about one-half mile over the city line to Elinor Place in Yonkers. We now lived in a different school district, and I could attend Gordon High School in Yonkers, but McBurney was where I belonged. There was no doubt in my mind that we had been led there by God. But not long after we moved, I heard from the kitchen, "Well, I'm not going to tell him. You'll have to do it," and then Dad walked into the living room.

"Have a seat, Bob," Dad said as he sat on the couch across the room from me. He leaned forward and clasped his hands in front of him with his elbows on his knees.

"You know how hard it is for us to earn enough money for expenses. Well, I'm afraid it's not going to be possible to raise the tuition for McBurney. You're going to have to go to Gordon High School."

"Okay, Dad," was all I said. I went upstairs to my room and lay down on my bed with my hands clasped under my head. I was stunned. God! It was so disappointing!

After awhile, I heard footsteps coming up the stairs. My mother came in. "I'm so sorry it has come to this," she said as she sat on the edge of my bed.

"I really thought I was going to McBurney, Mom. I mean, has Daddy known all the time? Why let me get my hopes up?" I struggled hard not to let the tears flow.

She sat for a few seconds and then said, "You must make a real effort to know, right now, deep down in your heart, that you are God's perfect child. I know you understand it in theory. But now you must know it in your heart. You must also know that Daddy is God's child. So am I. Because of that, we all are being cared for by God. God is in control. Daddy's not in control. I'm not in control. You're not in control. Neither is money in control. You must trust God to put you where you belong."

"But, Mom, why do we have to go through this? Why can't we just know where I'm going to go? Why did Daddy wait until now to tell me?"

"Perhaps Daddy was hoping that somehow the money would become available. I don't know. But I do know that we have to let things unfold in God's time. Right now, at this instant, you are exactly where you belong—in this house, in your room, on your bed. Four weeks from now, you also will be exactly where you belong. God's plan for you will have unfolded. And you will know that it is God's plan, and you will be satisfied."

I did attend McBurney. Many years later my mother told me she had saved the tuition by squeezing a bit more for the mortgage than we actually needed out of my father and by saving her own earnings from her fledgling practice as a Christian Science practitioner. I had not paid much attention to the fact that she had become a practitioner. I only knew that every now and then some woman would call on my mother in our home. These ladies would visit quite regularly—sometimes weekly. It never occurred to me that they paid her. But they did. And their payments helped make it possible for me to go to McBurney.

PEEKSKILL

It was Labor Day—Monday, Sept. 5, 1949.

I had spent the weekend with my cousins in Leonia, New Jersey, just across the Hudson River from Manhattan. My cousin John and I were both fifteen years old and about to start our sophomore years—he at Leonia High School, and I at McBurney.

While we were having lunch on Monday afternoon, the telephone rang. Uncle Leroy went into the living room to answer it. After a few minutes he returned to the table. "That was your father, Bob," he said. "Seems he and your mother have had a rather bad time of it."

"Were they in an accident?" Aunt Dorothy asked.

"I couldn't say. He didn't want to talk about it. Said they'd fill us in when they get here, but they're both okay." Uncle Leroy looked at me and John and his voice lightened, "What are you two going to do with yourselves this afternoon?"

"I dunno," John responded.

"I have an idea," Uncle Leroy said as he turned to me. "Have you seen how we work with the bees?"

"No," I said.

Uncle Leroy had several beehives way at the back of their yard.

"Would you like to give me a hand at it?" he asked.

"Yeah. Sure."

"All right then. After we finish here, I'll don my bee togs, and we can go out to the hives. It's quite interesting. That ought to keep us busy until your parents get here."

We spent the rest of the afternoon helping my uncle remove honeycomb frames from the hives, replace them with new frames, and then extract the honey. I had the feeling my uncle wanted to make sure I was kept busy so I wouldn't worry.

Soon after we had finished and gone back into the house, I heard the back door open and Aunt Dorothy exclaim, "Well here you are! My goodness. We were beginning to worry. I'm glad you're here. You're just in time for dinner."

"Hello, Dot," I heard my father say. "Yes, we're here. Where's Bob?"

"He and John are in the living room. Why don't you go on in?"

John and I were playing gin rummy. I was sitting with my back to the wall and could see my father and mother behind John as they came into the room.

"Hello boys," Dad said. My mother didn't say anything. But her face was almost stony with a haunted expression.

"Hi," I said as I got up and walked toward them. "Are you okay?" I kissed my father on the cheek, and then went to my mother. She gave me a long, hard hug and kissed me on the cheek. Then she held on to my shoulders, pushed me back, and stared at me.

"Well. Yes. We're fine. Physically," Dad said. "But your mother and I have been through an horrendous experience."

"Why? What happened?" I asked. My mother dropped her hands, and I turned to Dad.

"We were caught in a terrible riot. I wouldn't be surprised if someone was killed. But why don't we wait until we're together at dinner, and we can tell you about it then."

Soon all of us were seated around Aunt Dorothy's dining room table. We bowed our heads and Uncle Leroy said grace. Then he said, "Well, James. Why don't you fill us in?"

"Yes. Well … Katherine and I decided to take a trip up north into Westchester. It's beautiful country up there." We all nodded. "And we thought it would be fun to hike and hitchhike, go wherever opportunities allowed us. We walked north until we found ourselves at the Saw Mill River Parkway. We quickly hitched a ride, which brought us to Ossining, NY. Our driver lived in town and drove us to a guest house where we decided to stay since it was getting dark. The next morning, after breakfast, Katherine saw an ad for a concert by Paul Robeson[1] in the local newspaper. Another couple staying at the guest house was going to the concert so they took us. The concert took place on a golf course with a large outdoor amphitheater-type area. Some twenty-five thousand people were there."

"The concert was quite nice," Mother said. "Paul Robeson sang several songs and arias. He was magnificent, and there were other performers."

My father said that at the end of the concert it was announced that no one was to leave the concert area on foot. So, the couple who had brought them to the

---

1.   Paul Robeson was one of the first Black civil rights activists during the strident era of McCarthyism. He also was a Broadway actor, athlete and bass concert singer.

concert loaded them, along with two other people, into their car. "It was a very crowded car," Dad said.

"And we were warned not to open our windows," my mother added. "Can you imagine that? It was very hot outside, and the car became like an oven."

"We were not allowed to exit the way we came in," Dad explained. "Instead we were directed down a narrow dirt road, which was lined with thousands of men wearing American Legion uniforms and armed with baseball bats and rocks.

"Suddenly, these hoodlums were throwing rocks at us and smashing the cars with their bats. The cars could move only very slowly and spasmodically." As I looked at my father I saw that his face had turned red. "The police just stood by. I saw some of them actually grinning. One policeman even poked his billy club into a passenger-side car window, right at a woman's face. He did it right in front of us. It was ghastly."

"Did they strike you? Were you hurt?" Uncle Leroy asked.

"No. One rear, side window was smashed. The woman next to Katherine got some glass in her face. But she appeared to be basically all right."

Then my mother looked toward me, "I must say, I've never prayed as hard as I prayed during that horrible hour-long gauntlet of angry men with bats, sticks, and rocks."

Dad continued, "And you should have heard what they were shouting at us—things like, 'Hey, you white niggers, go back to Russia,' or 'Jew, Jew, go back to Jew town. We'll finish Hitler's job!' I mean why did we fight the war? Or they shouted 'Give us Robeson! We'll string that nigger up! Come back again, and we'll kill you!' It was unbelievable. I've heard that stuff coming out of the South. But up here in the North?"

"But what brought this on, James?" Aunt Dorothy asked.

Dad explained that their driver and his wife had come to the concert from the city, as had the third couple in the car. After they broke out of the concert grounds, he offered to take them home. On the way, he told them that the locals were apparently of the opinion that the area had become a summer haven for New York City communists.

"And this morning on the radio, we heard the Westchester County District Attorney—Fanelli is his name—praise the police for doing a magnificent job. Good God! Then Gov. Dewey came on and said that we concertgoers were members of communist groups who provoked the riot. Katherine and I are communists? What's he talking about? This was a concert, for God's sake. That's all Katherine and I went to. There were thousands of women and children in the crowd and in the cars. Hundreds of them were pummeled and beaten. It was one of the most disgusting things I have ever seen."

"But where did this happen, Dad?"

"Peekskill! Peekskill, New York. You know, this right wing bullying can't go on. This was a flagrant violation of the First Amendment. The police, the district attorney, and the governor of the state of New York allowed these so-called veterans to bludgeon people because they didn't like what they believed. Something has to be done. This is after all America. I don't know about the rest of you, but I cannot sit idly by."

I looked across the table at my mother. Her eyes moved from my dad to me. I suddenly believed I understood. She was not haunted because of the riots. No. It was Dad. I looked at him. He had expressed anger while describing what they had seen. But now he was staring into space, and his mouth was grim. But he turned toward me, and his eyes showed that he was excited, even ecstatic.

As soon as we returned home, my father wrote a letter to the *Yonkers Herald Statesman* in which he complained bitterly about the way he and the other concertgoers had been mistreated and how the First Amendment to the Bill of Rights had been violated by the authorities.

He then joined the Westchester Committee for Human Rights. Soon after, he joined that organization's board of directors. Shortly after that, he and others formed the Yonkers Committee for Peace. He was elected president.

He told me, "We're attempting to stem the tide of reactionary thinking that's sweeping the country and trying to smother the Bill of Rights—the kind of actions we saw at Peekskill; the kind of actions that we see coming out of the House Un-American Activities Committee; and the kind of actions backed by Senator McCarthy and his blacklists. We're attempting to stem all of it."

My mother told me that Dad had finally found his religion.

BUCK HILL FALLS

In January of 1951, I and four other juniors from McBurney attended a religious conference at Buck Hill Falls in the Pocono mountains in Pennsylvania. As far as I knew, I was the only Christian Scientist present.

We were mingling with two to three hundred other teenagers, all juniors, from various schools throughout the metropolitan New York area. We had been told that this was to be an "enriching" experience—an opportunity to get some understanding of how others thought and what they believed. It was also supposed to be an opportunity for us to gain some sense of respect for others' beliefs. Presumably, then, it would be my responsibility to explain Christian Science to all these strangers.

◆　　　◆　　　◆

"So, how does Christian Science work?" Rebecca, a cute young woman of fifteen or sixteen years of age, asked me. We had broken up into small groups with no adults present. We were four boys and three girls, sitting or standing in one section of the very large meeting room that had been our dining room last night. I was standing and leaning on a door jamb looking down at Rebecca as she and the others looked back at me.

During the previous night's general assembly in the dining room, we had been told that there were three basic religious groups present at this meeting: Catholics, Protestants and Jews. I claimed membership in the Protestant group because I did believe in Jesus, but I wasn't a Catholic. Jews, it seemed, believed in the same God as the rest of us, but they didn't believe that Jesus was the son of God.

I, too, had been taught that Jesus was the son of God. But I also had been taught that *all* of us, not just Jesus, were sons and daughters of God. The Catholics and Protestants seemed to be saying that not only was Jesus *the* son of God but that he also was "God incarnate," which meant that God had walked on earth in the body of Jesus. I had never heard of such a thing. The Christians also said that to be a Christian meant that you accepted the Trinity—the Father, the Son, and the Holy Spirit, which were somehow three and one at the same time.

David and Rebecca, who were both Jewish, looked at each other with puzzled eyes. I, too, was puzzled and thought that perhaps they could see it in my eyes. I suddenly felt a kind of kinship with them. I thought that I was a Christian. Christian Scientists followed Jesus' teachings, I believed. Still, I felt myself wishing I could be as secure in my faith as Rebecca seemed to be in her faith as a Jew, whether or not I fit the Christian mold as far as the Trinity was concerned.

Now, Rebecca had turned to me with her question.

"Well," I said, "we also believe in Jesus. And we believe in all of his miracles, but we don't call them miracles."

"You don't?" someone piped up.

"No. We believe that Jesus knew how to heal because he was so spiritual."

"You mean he could get God to do these things?" another boy asked.

"No, not really. It was more like he knew the laws of God so well that he could use God's laws to heal." I continued, "You believe that God is infinite. Right?"

They nodded.

"And you believe that God is perfect?"

"Yes," several responded.

"Then if God is perfect and God is infinite, how can there be any sickness?" They stared at me not quite getting it. "That's what Jesus knew when he looked at a sick person. Where you and I might see a sick person, he saw God's perfect child. That's how he healed people."

I saw a light of understanding, if not belief, dawn in the eyes of several of my fellow workshop attendees. Then we moved on to questions of other members. Rebecca was asked to explain why Jews didn't believe in Jesus. Then a Lutheran was asked to explain his beliefs, a Catholic his, and a Presbyterian his. It became rather confusing to me. There were so many interpretations of the meaning of God and our relationship to him.

But at least my role as a representative Christian Scientist had ended. It was okay. I felt good. These teenagers hadn't seemed to think my beliefs were particularly strange. But the confusion in my thought that materialized at that conference lingered for many years. "How could so many beliefs exist in so many people regarding the same God?" I asked myself. "It is the same God. Isn't it?"

PEACE

On Monday night, Nov. 19, 1951, I stood along the wall of the auditorium of the YWCA at 75 S. Broadway in Yonkers. My father sat in the center of the front row. He was chatting with the man sitting on his left. My mother sat on his right. She stared straight ahead. I knew she was knowing the truth, knowing that no harm could come tonight.

The place was packed. I was scared out of my wits.

No amount of knowing the truth on my part could dispel my fear. The *Yonkers Herald Statesman* had run a page one article on Saturday afternoon announcing that the police and veterans groups were doing everything that they could to shut down this forum, which was being sponsored by the Yonkers Committee for Peace. My father had asked me to usher.

Men filled the seats. Some had their Army uniforms on, some wore American Legion hats. For all I knew some of these guys had beaten the concertgoers at Peekskill.

Finally, one of the two men sitting on the platform got up from his chair.

"Good evening ladies and gentlemen," the man said. "Thank you all for coming. My name is Dr. James Fleming, and I have been asked to chair this forum. We are most fortunate to have Stephen G. Cary speak to us this evening." He looked in the direction of the second man sitting on the platform. "Mr. Cary," he continued, "is a member of the American Friends Service Committee. He chaired the AFSC committee, which published a report called 'Steps to Peace. A Quaker View of United States Foreign Policy.' Mr. Cary is going to explain that report to us."

Dr. Fleming announced that there would be a question-and-answer period following Mr. Cary's talk. He said questions had to be submitted in writing, and he would read all questions before giving them to Mr. Cary. Only those having to do with Mr. Cary's speech would be answered.

Polite applause greeted Mr. Cary as he rose to speak.

Nothing Mr. Cary said caused any commotion even though everything he said was similar to things I had heard from my father. How many times had I heard Dad say that U.S. foreign policy was based mainly on military force? Or that all the money that was being spent on the military would be better spent improving the education and welfare of people around the world. Or that the United States wasn't trying hard enough to come to a disarmament agreement with the Soviets. These all were Dad's favorite themes.

I knew that the men at this meeting believed that the Soviets were trying to take over the world, and there should be no negotiating with them.

Then the question-and-answer period started. The audience listened quietly while Mr. Fleming read questions to Mr. Cary until Mr. Fleming rejected a question saying, "This question is not pertinent to Mr. Cary's speech, and therefore, it will not be answered."

Suddenly some guy in the back of the auditorium leaped to his feet and yelled that if a question was to be read it should be answered.

Dr. Fleming said, "Nobody objected to the procedure when I outlined it, and I have kept faith."

This caused the man in back to yell louder and a bunch of the veterans to start hooting, but the rest of the audience drowned them out with applause.

Then another man jumped up in the rear, ran to the platform, and demanded that a question he had addressed to *my father* be read and answered.

Dr. Fleming again explained that because the question was not about Mr. Cary's speech it would not be answered. A whole bunch of people applauded while another bunch booed. Finally the guy returned to his seat.

Mr. Cary answered two more questions, and the forum was closed. Everyone filed out peacefully.

◆   ◆   ◆

"Well. That wasn't so bad, was it?" my father asked as we drove home.

"I guess not," I answered. "Who was that guy who did all the objecting?"

"Oh that was Emmett Burke. He's that city councilman who's been raising all kinds of objections. He's one of the leaders of the veterans—a real reactionary."

"But it didn't make sense, Dad. I thought they didn't want any controversy."

"Goes to show you, doesn't it? What they wanted was an excuse to shut us down in flagrant violation of our First Amendment right to free speech. I wouldn't be at all surprised if they planted that question. You can see that we had to be very careful not to give those hoodlums any excuse for acting like they did at Peekskill."

◆　　◆　　◆

On Tuesday evening, the *Herald Statesman* reported on its front page:

Burke Booed As He Interrupts Two-Hour Peace Forum At Y

In editorials, the newspaper had always favored the veterans. After Peekskill, they had praised the police and the State Attorney General. This had incensed my father, and he wrote complaint letters to the *Statesman*. But to me, this article seemed to tell things as they had happened, and even to show Burke and the veterans in their true colors.

Two days later on page two, the headline read:

Council Of Churches Praises Y.W.C.A., 'Repudiates' Censors Raps Protests By 'Ill-Advised Groups' And Calls on 33 Member Churches To Be Alert On Freedoms

"All right. We're getting somewhere," Dad said. "Now maybe one of them will host our next forum."

But when asked, the churches said that they regretted that their membership was unwilling to have the Yonkers Committee for Peace conduct a forum in their place of worship.

"Doesn't surprise me in the least," Dad said. "They're all scared to death. But we're not going to give up."

Not long after this meeting, the Yonkers Committee for Peace applied to the Yonkers Board of Education for permission to hold another forum in one of the public schools. They were denied. They appealed all the way to the U.S. Supreme Court.

Until Peekskill, I saw my father as a typical dad—gentle, loving, practical. Now, I saw an entirely new father—a man who religiously believed in the principles he espoused. My mother was troubled by Dad's activities. They threatened her relationships with her patients and fellow church members. "What will people think?" she asked me. I also found his activities scary. But, in hindsight, I came to see my father as a hero.

A PRACTITIONER

In the spring of 1953, I was attending Swarthmore College outside of Philadelphia, Pennsylvania. I was nearing the end of my freshmen year. My mother telephoned and asked me to find a practitioner for myself.

"Here's why," she explained. "I am your mother. You are my son. That is a very special relationship. But now you have become an adult, and I am finding it difficult to let go of my sense of our relationship so I can be completely objective in my thinking about you as a patient. Will you think about it?"

"Yeah. Okay."

"I detect some hesitancy," she said. "Are you reluctant to turn to another practitioner? Or are you beginning to question your understanding in Christian Science?"

"Somehow, I don't believe I'm wondering about my understanding in Christian Science," I replied. "It's true that from day to day I hardly ever talk about Christian Science to anyone. But there are a few of us on the campus, plus one professor. We've formed a CS Org.[1] We meet every Tuesday evening. In fact, I have to do the readings for the next one. We rotate the job."

"That's wonderful. Why haven't you told me?"

"I didn't think there was anything special about it. I also probably should tell you that I've been going to a lot of Quaker meetings on Sundays."

"Why not the Christian Science church in Swarthmore?"

"That's about a mile–and-a-half walk. The meeting house is right on campus. But I have to admit, I sometimes feel like I get more out of the Quaker meetings than the church service."

"And why would that be?"

"Well. You know the Quaker meetings are sort of like the last half of one of our Wednesday meetings. The Quakers believe in what they call the 'inner light.' That inner light is what's supposed to cause them to speak. Everybody comes in,

---

1.   Christian Science Organization–These college campus organizations are founded under the auspices of the Mother Church in Boston. Their meetings are modeled after branch church Wednesday meetings.

sits down, and stays quiet until someone feels an urge to stand up and say something."

"Like a testimony."

"Well, yeah. But, for the most part, people don't have a lot to say about God. Lately, it's all been about McCarthy or the cold war. Most Quakers are pacifists, you know. They don't like the military build up, and they hate the nuclear arms race."

"And you find this sort of thing more inspirational than what you might hear in a Christian Science church? You're sounding like your father."

"No. It's not that. Although I have to say that Dad would love to hear what these folks have to say. The thing is, there are a couple of people who almost always manage to speak toward the end of the meeting and bring everybody back to where they were supposed to be. One man speaks of Divine Love or Divine Mind and how we need to allow ourselves to be led by them. I always sit up when he speaks.

"But can you explain to me why you find the Quaker meetings more satisfying for you than the services downtown?"

"I'm not sure, except to say that I think maybe I find the Quaker meetings sort of reassuring. Hearing one's own beliefs supported by someone outside of one's own religious persuasion is helpful."

"This is quite wonderful, Bob. You've heard me say many times that we Christian Scientists have no monopoly on the truth of being. What you're now saying proves it. We do find evidence in all sorts of places. It can be quite comforting, can't it?"

"I have to admit, it can."

"This also says to me that you're attempting to find your own understanding. And that brings me back to the reason for my call. It's time for you to find someone outside of your family to whom you can turn."

"Okay. A couple of people's names have come to me."

"Well, don't tell me who they are. Let it be your own demonstration."

"Okay. Thanks Mom," I said before we hung up.

Until that moment I had given no thought whatsoever to the idea of locating a Christian Science practitioner for myself. Most Christian Scientists face this problem at some point. My mother had. She had found Agnes Davis who had a large practice in New York City. Mother had visited her frequently. And my mother had developed her own practice in our home. When Mrs. Davis retired and moved to California, she turned her practice over to my mother. So Mother now commuted daily to her office on West Forty-second Street, which used to be Mrs. Davis's office.

"So what is a proper practitioner?" I had to ask myself. "Exactly what is it you will be looking for when you try to find the right person? What sort of problems will you expect to solve with this person's assistance? How might such a person work with you? Where will you look for this person?"

The answer to the last question was easy in theory. The *Christian Science Journal* was a monthly publication that included articles on Christian Science and gave various authors' insights. In the last pages of each issue was a listing of all the Christian Science practitioners in the world. You could look a person up by country and then by city. Every practitioner's name, address, and telephone number was listed. I looked up the United States, Pennsylvania, and then the town of Swarthmore. I found three listings for people who probably were members of the local church and who would be glad to have me call them.

Most people thought of practitioners as being healers. In a way, that was a correct definition. But what did they heal? And how did they heal?

The "what" could be any issue that might be confronting a person, from problems with personal relationships, to employment issues, to difficulties in understanding course material. And the need to cure a bad cold could arise.

How they healed was a question of the practitioner helping the patient gain a better understanding of his particular situation in light of his relationship to God. When I found myself panicking over an upcoming examination, the standard answer was to understand that there was only one Mind. That Mind was God. That Mind was the only intelligence operating. That Mind was my mind. As long as I had taken all the proper human footsteps in the way of attending classes, taking notes, and studying appropriately, I could leave it up to Mind to give me the answers to that test. But, in the face of a sense of panic, it could be difficult to see such an analysis. The right practitioner could help a person understand his situation correctly by reminding him of his relationship to God or Divine Mind—all intelligent, all knowledgeable—thus ridding the patient of the panic. And then the practitioner would pray for his patient silently during the following days to support him until his problem had been met. Knowing that my mother was standing with me was very helpful.

Now, I had to find someone to fill her shoes. Calling on some stranger in Swarthmore didn't appeal to me. I could think of only two people. Both were my Sunday school teachers at Fifth Church of Christ, Scientist, in Manhattan. When I started attending high school at McBurney, my mother had decided we should find a large city church where we could find a Sunday school that had men teaching the high school students. My regular teacher had been Mr. Parsons, a former FBI agent who now worked as an executive with a large chemical corporation headquartered in Manhattan. When he couldn't teach, our substitute teacher was Mr. Hudson. He was a full-time practitioner. I knew and respected both men well.

In Sunday school, we tended to deal with the normal issues facing teenage boys. Various questions would be raised, and we all would be asked to describe how we might think about these issues in Christian Science. I knew from these discussions that nothing was new to my teachers. They had heard it all before. Their advice and counseling could be trusted. Mr. Hudson was a Journal-listed practitioner. I telephoned him.

◆   ◆   ◆

Some six weeks later my mother telephoned. "I couldn't stand it any longer. I haven't heard from you in quite some time. It's as though you dropped off the edge of the earth. I have to know how you're doing," she said.

"Oh, well, I didn't think you wanted me to bother you anymore."

"It wasn't that I didn't want you to bother me. It was that I felt you needed someone other than me to serve as your practitioner. You do see the difference. Don't you?"

"Yeah. I do. I'm sorry, Mom. It's been really busy here. I'm studying for exams and all."

"Well, I know I said I didn't want to interfere with your demonstration, but I have to ask. Have you found a practitioner?"

"Oh, yeah. Sure. I called Mr. Hudson."

"Oh, for heaven's sake. I chat with him quite frequently. His office is just down the hall from mine."

"I know."

"And he never said anything."

"Well he wouldn't. Would he?"

"No. You're right. Of course he wouldn't. I must admit I was getting anxious. But, of course, I had no reason to. It was just a mother's concern. I'm glad you've worked things out."

◆   ◆   ◆

I continued attending Quaker meetings rather frequently while at Swarth-more. I felt that the Quaker reliance on the "inner light" lent credence to my own understanding in Christian Science. As well, the fair play/free speech Quaker atmosphere supported my sense of what Dad was doing.

THE SUPREME COURT
OF THE UNITED STATES

At 11:00 one night in the fall of 1954, my father telephoned me from Yonkers. I had just hit the sack in my dorm at Swarthmore College, where I was a junior.

"Bob, the case against the Yonkers Board of Education is coming before the Supreme Court tomorrow morning. I'm going to Washington DC to hear it."

He said that he would be catching the Baltimore & Ohio train from Jersey City. It would arrive in Philadelphia at 3:00 AM, and I could join him there.

◆　　　◆　　　◆

At 3:00 AM, after taking the last train into Philadelphia from Swarthmore, I got on Dad's train and found him sitting alone on a spacious two-person seat. Another spacious seat faced him. We greeted each other as I sat. I was feeling strangely nervous and guilty. This case had to be extremely important to my father, yet I had not kept track of it. I asked, "So, how long have you been pursuing this case? It must be around four years."

"Just about," he replied.

"Dad, there's something I've never been able to ask you." I paused for a second, unsure of how to phrase my question. Then I blurted out, "I can't help but wonder what drives you—chairing the Yonkers Committee for Peace, writing all those letters to the newspapers, and you do it all in the face of tremendous opposition, even hatred. Why do you do it?"

He turned his gaze back out the window. "It's something I ask myself from time to time. Your mother says it's as though I've discovered a religion of some kind. I don't know. Maybe she's right." There was a long pause. Then he continued, "I enjoy the people I'm working with—most especially the ACLU[1] and their attorney, Emanuel Redfield. I must admit that I did *not* enjoy having a stone come through our window. You heard about that didn't you?" He looked at me.

1.　American Civil Liberties Union

"Yeah. Mom told me. She was scared to death."

"I know she was. Somehow I wasn't. It just steeled my resolve." He looked back at the window. "I also found being interviewed by the FBI quite motivating."

"The FBI?"

"Yes. Two tall, blond, all-America type FBI agents came to the house. I entertained them in the downstairs foyer," he said with a slight twinkle in his eye. "They quizzed me about the committee. I thought the whole thing was a stupid waste of time. They asked me if I would defend the United States if it were attacked. 'Of course I would,' I responded. 'You don't understand, do you? I'm fighting for our most basic rights—*your* most basic rights—as citizens of the United States.'

"'What rights?' they asked. "'*What rights!?*' I replied rhetorically. 'Our rights under the Bill of Rights of the Constitution of our nation—freedom of speech, freedom of assembly. You're not going to tell me the FBI is opposed to the Bill of Rights, are you?'"

"'No. We're not,' they said.

"'Well then,' was all I said. And they thanked me and left our house. But it gave me pause. How can we have gotten to the point where our nation is so embroiled in this anti-communist hysteria that we've thrown out the Bill of Rights? I mean, they have government and corporate employees signing loyalty oaths. What on earth did we fight the Second World War for? So we could have our own fascist government? That's what's at stake, you know. If the McCarthys and the Nixons in our government have their way, we'll end up with a dictatorship."

"But do you deny that the Soviet Union is threatening us?" I asked.

"I suppose not. But my point would be, where's the threat here?" He pointed at the floor. "Are you trying to tell me that the Yonkers Committee for Peace is a threat to the security of the United States of America, the strongest nation in the history of mankind? Are we such a threat that we can't speak on the subject of *peace* in a public forum? Now I ask you, if we can't hold a meeting because the subject of peace might be controversial, is that not a crucial violation of the First Amendment? I'm trusting that the Court will agree."

"Do you think they will?"

"Hard to tell. Emanuel thinks we have a chance. In spite of all the McCarthyism, the Supreme Court is not totally conservative. We have Warren, Black, and Douglas—good, down-to-earth liberals. That's three. You need five justices to win. So we have to convince two more. Clark has been known to go both ways. So he might be a fourth. The question is can we convince one more?"

I had always thought of my father as the hard-working, practical, do-it-yourself man. And recently I thought of him as a guardian of civil rights. But at this instant, he was giving me a thoughtful analysis of the make-up of the U.S. Supreme Court. It was fascinating.

◆   ◆   ◆

Shortly after 6:00 AM, our train pulled into Union Station in Washington DC. As we worked our way out of the car and down the platform, Dad said, "There's Emanuel." We exchanged greetings, had breakfast, and at 9:30 AM the three of us walked up the broad marble steps of the Supreme Court building and entered the Great Hall.

We followed Emanuel as he walked straight ahead, turned a corner, and then entered a suite of very elegantly furnished offices. A pleasant looking woman rose from her desk when she saw us.

"Hello Mr. Redfield," she said. "Just one moment please." She went into another office. Soon she and a man returned.

"Hello, Mr. Redfield," the man said.

Mr. Redfield introduced us to Mr. Edmondson, the clerk of the Supreme Court. Mr. Edmondson smiled, reached out, and shook our hands. "Welcome Gentlemen," he said. "Well, I know you need to get ready, Mr. Redfield, so why don't I show these gentlemen around while you take your leave."

I assumed that Mr. Edmondson knew what our case was about. Yet he seemed unconcerned that in many circles my father was considered a "pinko-stinko, fellow-traveler, communist sympathizer."

Mr. Edmondson led us out of his office area and gave us a brief tour. At 10:30 we entered the courtroom. We sat slightly to the right of the room and near the front. A few rows ahead of us, behind a railing, were desks and chairs at which Mr. Redfield and his opposing counsel sat. In the middle of this area was a lectern from which the attorneys addressed the court. Mr. Edmondson had explained that the lectern had a white light and a red light on it. The attorneys would be signaled with a white light when their allotted time was running out and with the red light when their time was over.

Suddenly, we were told to rise as the justices filed in behind their long desk. The Court Marshall called the case of Ellis et al vs. Dixon and the Board of Education of the City of Yonkers. I watched Mr. Redfield proceed to the rostrum. As

Mr. Redfield spoke, he was interrupted several times by the justices as they sought clarification of various points. Too soon, it seemed to me, the little warning light came on. Then the red light came on, and Mr. Redfield sat down. Then Dixon's attorney rose and pled his defense. He ran slightly over his time.

And it was over.

Out we went into the daylight. Mr. Redfield joined us a few minutes later on the courthouse steps. He had no idea how the decision was going to come down. He felt the questions from the justices appeared to go in Dad's favor. "But you never know," he said. It had been the more liberal justices, Warren, Douglas, and Black, who had asked what seemed to be the more telling questions. It would be several months before the decision was handed down.

◆   ◆   ◆

My father and I caught a 2:30 train that afternoon. We again found empty seats that faced each other. We leaned back and loosened our ties. "How do you feel about what happened?" I asked.

"Extremely interesting," he said. "How about yourself?"

"I think it has to be the most important experience I've ever had in my life. Think about it, Dad. We just saw your case, a case involving possibly the most important issue facing us today, argued before some of the most brilliant legal minds in the world. How many people have an experience like this? It's incredible."

"Mmm. I know. But, as brilliant as they may be, they also can be wrong. Never forget that, Bob. Intelligence does not spell rightness. They could vote against us."

"That's true. And I suppose there's no way you'd accept that as being correct."

"Absolutely not. If these were saner times, the school board would have had no problem allowing us to have our meeting. All kinds of organizations have meetings there. These are perilous times. If we are not careful, we stand a good chance of losing everything our nation was founded on. Today, whole segments of the population can't get jobs because they are suspected of having had something to do with an organization that advocates the violent overthrow of our, or any, government." He paused. Then he said, "Need I remind you that our government was *founded on the violent overthrow* of the then-existing government?" He paused for a second, looked away from me, and then looked back. "I'll never give up this fight, Bob; not so long as I have a breath in my body."

I had never heard my father speak so eloquently and passionately to me.

"So what will you do if the decision comes down against you?"

"We'll find some other way to hold our meeting. There is absolutely no reason why the school board should deny us our constitutional rights." He paused a moment, smiled, and said, "You know, Bob, we haven't had much sleep in the past twenty-four hours. I can hardly keep my eyes open."

We both leaned back in our seats. Dad closed his eyes. As I looked at him, I realized that I had never felt more proud of my father than I did at that instant. I left him in Philadelphia and returned to Swarthmore in time for dinner.

◆   ◆   ◆

On June 6, 1955, the Supreme Court handed down its six-page decision, which concluded that my father's claims were "too amorphous to permit adjudication of constitutional issues asserted," indicating that there was no proof that the Yonkers School Board had allowed other organizations *of like manner* to hold meetings. Mr. Chief Justice Warren, Mr. Justice Black, Mr. Justice Douglas, and Mr. Justice Clark dissented saying only that they believed "that the allegations of the petition are sufficient to state a case of discrimination under the Equal Protection Clause."

That same year, the Yonkers Committee for Peace again applied to the board of education for meeting space. Their application was again denied. The committee appealed. This time the New York Court of Appeals reversed the board, and the committee was able to hold its meeting.

Mom said Dad had found his religion. I supposed that the tenets of his religion were the Bill of Rights. My religion made it possible for me to believe that the founding fathers of our nation were quite literally divinely inspired. I never heard Dad speak of "divine" inspiration when speaking of the likes of Tom Paine, Thomas Jefferson et al. On the other hand, I knew he studied their writings assiduously. I suppose those writings were, in some way, his Bible.

I have often asked myself, "What then, in the last analysis, is religion?"

DAY ROOM

Fort Dix, New Jersey: The first Saturday afternoon in September of 1959.

We would not be allowed off the base until next weekend when we would complete our first four weeks of basic training. We had from noon on Saturday until Sunday evening off. Except for sleeping, we didn't dare stay in our barracks. We might get caught by some sergeant looking for a detail to clean the latrine or some such thing. So, the question always was, where could we hide during those precious daylight hours?

I had chosen our company's Day Room. It was a strange place to go. Normally, we stayed as far away from our company area as we could get. We did so purely for the purpose of avoiding any chance of being grabbed for a dreaded detail. But on this Saturday afternoon I had no desire to be with anyone. I felt utterly alone and somewhat desperate. It seemed that I had come to the end of the line. A few days ago, the *New York Times* had published a list of all those who had passed the New York State Bar Exam. My name was not on that list.

All of the guys in our company of one hundred twenty men had joined the Army National Guard in order to avoid the two-year draft. Our student deferments had run out. Therefore, we had chosen to enlist for six months of active duty to be followed by five and a half years of reserve duty. The two-year draftees and three-year enlistees called us "six-month wonders." Many of us had just finished graduate school. Quite a few, like myself, had graduated from law school. I did not notice how many others in my barracks had not passed the bar.

Reason told me that I should not be surprised. I had finished my third year of law school utterly exhausted from the preparation for and taking of my final exams at the University of Pennsylvania in Philadelphia. Then I had spent a month taking a New York State Bar review course. I felt as though I were in a sleepless trance. I was constantly telling myself I should have taken a few months off before attempting the bar. In the end, I had rushed through the exam, writing my answers hurriedly, even impatiently. I turned in my exam about three hours before everybody else and left the downtown Manhattan examination facility.

"So what did you expect?" I asked myself as I sat alone in the Day Room. "Yeah, I know. But ..." I answered myself. "So, now what do you do? What has it been all about? You've spent three years in law school believing that was where you belonged. Going there was, after all, a Christian Science demonstration. Wasn't it? I mean, why did you go to law school?"

It was a question I asked myself many times. When contemplating graduating from Swarthmore during my senior year, I had seemed at loose ends. I interviewed for several corporate jobs. None worked out. Many who graduated from Swarthmore went to graduate school. After much praying, it came to me that I should apply to law school at Penn. But other than having sympathy for my father's interest in broad constitutional issues, I was not driven to go into the law.

"Well, it will be an excellent education for you no matter what you end up doing," several people told me.

As my first year at law school was coming to a close, I was quite certain I would be flunking out. I didn't know what to do. I applied to enter the Navy Air Force, passed the exam, and then failed the physical because my eyes were tired. I had had little sleep the night before. Soon after, I passed my first-year exams. Apparently I was wrong to doubt. So, I stayed with the law for two more years even though I had no idea what I would do with a law degree.

"Stick with it," I said to myself many times during the next two years. "God will show you the way."

Now I was sitting in this Day Room., "What do I do, God?" I asked

I looked around the room. It looked rather like a library reading room. There were several upholstered armchairs, one of which I occupied. Quite a few books were on the shelves. Across the room was a newspaper rack. I walked over to the newspapers. There was a *New York Times*, a *New York Herald Tribune*, a *Philadelphia Inquirer* and, at the bottom, a four-week-old edition of the *Christian Science Monitor*. I lifted the *Monitor* out of the rack and returned to my chair.

Christian Science had been a source of great solace for me during the past four weeks. Privates during basic training have very little privacy. But I had my Bible and *Science and Health* with me, and I was able to steal a moment here and there for reading a phrase or two. And every Wednesday night I was given leave to go to a Christian Science service that was held on the base by a Christian Science chaplain in a small nondenominational chapel. It was a comfort to meet a few other guys who were in the same boat as myself. Now, to my surprise, I found this copy of the *Monitor*. I wondered how it had gotten there. Perhaps that chaplain had left it.

The news was old, but since I had not seen anything for the past four weeks, it was interesting. I randomly looked at various headlines and flipped from this page to that. Suddenly, my eyes focused on the classifieds, and I zeroed in on this ad:

> Copyboys. *Christian Science Monitor* newsroom.
> Candidates please write: Copyboy position
> The *Christian Science Monitor*
> One Norway Street, Boston, Massachusetts

The *Monitor* had recently been listed as the third best newspaper in the United States, behind the *New York Times* and the *St. Louis Post Dispatch*. One criteria for this rating had to do with how many Pulitzer prizes each publication had been awarded.

"Hmmm," I thought to myself, "is this why I came in here?" I had taken an elective course in writing at Swarthmore. I enjoyed sitting at a typewriter and turning out pieces, but I had never taken this interest seriously—until now. "Wouldn't it be something if you could become a reporter for the *Monitor*?" I asked myself.

Later that day, I dropped a letter addressed to the *Monitor* into the mail. Approximately two weeks later, I received an invitation from the *Monitor* to come to Boston for an interview. I wrote back that I would not be able to get there until Christmas leave. They responded that they would be happy to wait.

"This is it, then," I said to myself, even though I had not yet interviewed. I felt it in my bones. I was going to go to work for the *Christian Science Monitor* in Boston.

Upon completion of my eight weeks of basic training, I was shipped out to Fort Sill, Oklahoma—a long way from home and from Boston. As the time approached for our two weeks of Christmas leave, I had no money, and it seemed that I had no way to get back east. But I knew that I would be where I belonged, and I couldn't believe that place would be Fort Sill, Oklahoma.

About a week before the company area was to shut down for Christmas, two of my barracks mates asked me to help them drive to Cleveland. At a Howard Johnson's service area on the Ohio Turnpike, I met two lieutenants who were driving to Connecticut. They offered me a lift. They dropped me off at the exit for Broadway off the Henry Hudson Parkway. I walked down the exit ramp to Broadway. I was about one mile from home. I set down my duffel bag and stuck out my thumb. I was in uniform, and people did pick up soldiers. But none did on this dark, cold night.

I said to myself, "What are you doing, Ellis? God has brought you all this way, and now you're sticking out your thumb?" I picked up my bag and started walking toward home. After a few steps, I heard, "You look like you could use a lift, soldier." I looked to my left. A New York City patrol car carrying two officers had stopped next to me. A policeman was hanging his head out his window and looking at me.

"I sure could," I said.

"Where're you headed?" the driver asked.

I gave him my parents' address, and he said, "Hop in." These two policemen dropped me at the front door to my home.

I had not yet told my parents about my upcoming interview with the *Monitor*. When I did, soon after arriving home, my father asked, "What about the law?"

"I don't know. Maybe, if I get this job, I'll take the bar in Massachusetts. I have to admit, I'm at a loss right now. This is the only thing that has come to me."

"Humph," was his response.

Later, when I explained to my mother how the idea had come about she said, "It sounds like it could be a real working out—a real answer to your prayers. It'll be interesting to see where this takes you."

I always felt a sense of gratitude to those two New York City cops. They couldn't possibly have known it, but I fully believed that their decision to offer me a lift demonstrated perfectly the efficacy of trusting in God. I have given testimonies about that Christmas trip from Fort Sill to Yonkers many times at Wednesday evening meetings in various Christian Science churches.

I also had no doubt that the unsolicited ride they gave me helped me on a journey that would determine the course of the rest of my life, but it also led to an estrangement between my father and me.

THE MONITOR

On the last Monday of January 1960, I arrived at the *Christian Science Monitor* to start my new job as a copyboy.

During my two-week Christmas leave I had taken the bus to Boston, stayed in a YMCA overnight, and interviewed the next morning at the personnel department of the Christian Science Mother Church. The woman who interviewed me wondered if I wouldn't rather work in their legal department than for the *Monitor*. She suggested that I interview for both positions. I met with a Mr. Burke in the legal department. His office was like any other legal office—a room with a large desk and wall-to-wall shelves full of law books. He also thought it made more sense for me to work for his department than at the *Monitor*. I told him that I at least wanted to look into the *Monitor* before making any decision.

"Well. That's certainly understandable," he said. "Why don't you go on over there? If they ask you to come on board, give it a try for six months. If, after that time, you decide you'd like to give us a try, let me know."

I thanked him very much and went across the street to the *Monitor* offices. I was interviewed by Mr. Coyle, editor of the city desk. He sat at a desk in the middle of a large newsroom. Men and women sat typing at several desks in the room. Three men sat at a circular desk in the middle of the room.

"They're copy editors," Mr. Coyle explained. "They're checking the copy that these reporters have written before sending it off to the typesetters." He waved his hand over all the reporters I had noticed.

He introduced me to Dana Gatlin, a copyboy who had started a few weeks ago and had him give me a tour. I was introduced to many of the men and women who sat at the various desks. I also was introduced to the editors of American News, Foreign News, Travel, Arts and Entertainment, and other departments. Finally, I met very briefly Erwin D. Canham, editor in chief and one of the most famous newsmen of the time. An excited hum of conversation filled the place. Every now and then I'd hear a burst of laughter. People were coming and going. All were extremely cordial and welcoming.

Dana took me out to the pressroom. It was a huge, three-story room filled with machinery.

"What's that smell?" I asked.

"It's the ink. I love that smell. You will too," Dana said. "Wait till you see those machines running and the papers coming off the presses. There's nothing like it."

There was no contest. I told Mr. Coyle that I'd be mustered out of the Army toward the end of January. He asked me to come to work as quickly as I could after that.

Now, on this first day of work at the *Monitor*, I went to lunch with a couple of my fellow copyboys, including Dana Gatlin, in the small cafeteria. As we sat at our table, a gal in a very well filled out sweater and a flowing skirt swished by. "Who's that?" I asked.

"Forget about her." Dana answered. "That's Barbara Wemyss.[1] She's practically married to one of the richest guys in Boston. You'll never get anyplace with her."

I had to assume that she was a Christian Scientist since, as far I knew, everyone at the *Monitor* was. I had never dated anyone who was CS.[2] Dating non-Christian Scientists had been a problem for me. Almost invariably, parents objected to the idea of their daughter having anything to do with a Christian Scientist. But now in this totally CS environment I was staring as unobtrusively as I could at a very sexy but apparently unavailable CS gal.

◆　　◆　　◆

One month later I was fully absorbed in my job as a copyboy, and I was aspiring to become a *Monitor* staff writer. I was sharing an apartment with Dana and two other guys, and I had started dating Nicole Parkman, an assistant to the travel editor.

Soon thereafter, I went skiing for my first time with Dana, Nicole and several other people from the Mother Church. Toward the end of the day, I took a bad spill.

My left leg hurt like hell, but it didn't seem to be broken. We headed to the car with me hobbling mostly on my right leg. I sat in the back with my leg on the seat. When we got home, I hobbled up the stairs to our third-floor apartment and collapsed on my bed. The pain was excruciating. I knew I needed help.

1.　Pronounced Weems
2.　The acronym we all used when referring to Christian Science or Christian Scientists.

When I left Swarthmore and went to the University of Pennsylvania Law School in Philadelphia, I decided I should make Philadelphia my home for my three years of law school. I joined First Church of Christ, Scientist, in Philly, and located a local practitioner. She helped me through many crises. As always, the message was, "God knows where you belong."

When I arrived in Boston, I once again found myself in a new community. I again located a local practitioner. She had been recommended to me by Nicole.

I called my practitioner at 1:00 AM, and she said she would work with me. Finally, at about 2:00 AM, after receiving many calls from me, my practitioner noted that Mrs. Eddy said it was okay to have bones set by a doctor. "Perhaps," she suggested, "you should have it x-rayed."

Dana called a taxi and helped me get to the emergency room at Massachusetts General Hospital. I was told I had a "butterfly break" but that the bones were in good position. They put my leg in a cast up to my hip and sent me upstairs.

The next morning, I told a social worker that I wanted to leave and convalesce at the Christian Science Benevolent Association at Chestnut Hill. The BA was a Christian Science nursing home where Christian Scientists could receive basic nursing care while waiting for their healing. The social worker remonstrated with me, but I told her I wanted to be in a Christian Science atmosphere during my convalescence. I assured her that I would come back to Mass General for checkups. She agreed and an ambulance took me to the BA.

I had never seen the BA before. Now, as the ambulance pulled up, I beheld a large, Gothic style, stone mansion covered in ivy and set on the top of a beautifully landscaped estate. The approach to the building climbed the hill through thick but clearly manicured woods. The circular drive around which we drove to the building was filled with plantings, which probably would be in full bloom later in the spring.

The ambulance backed up to the entrance. Two nurses in crisp, white uniforms helped the ambulance attendants bring me in. I was set in a wheelchair with my leg propped up and sticking out in front, and the ambulance departed. The nurses cheerfully introduced themselves. They then wheeled me onto an elevator, took me up one floor, and pushed me down a long, carpeted hallway to what was to be my private room for some eight weeks.

The interior of the building, including my room, was equally as elegant as the exterior.

"What the hell am I going to do?" I wondered to myself as I lay on my back with my leg in the air. I had only started work at the *Christian Science Monitor*. How would I pay for anything?

A representative from the BA came into my room, pulled up a chair, and interviewed me. A few hours later she returned and told me that the *Monitor* would continue to pay me my weekly salary of forty-nine dollars, and the BA would charge me forty-nine dollars per week for my stay. The BA would also forgive me that payment for one week each month so I would be able to pay my rent, which also was forty-nine dollars per month. For this forty-nine dollars per week I would receive all my meals and all the nursing care I needed. I also would be transported by taxi to the Mass General clinic for my weekly appointments. I was grateful beyond words and I told her so.

I settled into my convalescence. In spite of all its elegance, the place was wonderfully friendly. I came to know the nurses and staff quite well. When I first arrived, meals were brought to my room. But soon, I was able to use my wheelchair to join the other patients in the dining room. I regularly attended Christian Science services, which were conducted in the chapel every Sunday and Wednesday. I did a lot of reading. Dana brought me my portable typewriter, and I attempted to do some writing.

Finally, the doctors at Mass General announced that they thought I was ready to get around on crutches. It was with a slight sense of regret that I returned to my apartment and to work.

But work I did. I became a full-fledged staff writer with the byline of Robert Y. Ellis. I was given the health, welfare and religion beat. Because of my law degree, I also was given special assignments to cover various court proceedings and to write commentary on decisions that were handed down by appeals courts. I became very familiar with many of the haunts that were frequented by reporters from the major dailies and radio stations. I was having a blast.

BARBARA

Around the first of the following November, Nicole announced that she was going to go to England. A bunch of us held a going away party for her, for which I borrowed some LP records from Barbara's roommate. The next morning I telephoned Barbara to find out how I could reach her roommate to return the records. She replied, "I like that. You call me to get my roommate's phone number?"

I responded, "Well, since I have you on the phone, what are you doing tonight?"

"I'm taking my dog to his weekly obedience class. Would you like to come?"

I nearly fell out of my chair, but I managed to say, "Yeah. That would be great."

That night, I joined Barbara and her toy poodle at obedience class. Barbara and her dog paraded around the classroom along with a lot of other people and their dogs. Charlie Brown was a bright, black, slightly oversized toy poodle—almost a mini. Barbara looked spectacularly snazzy as she pranced around the room telling him to sit, stay, and come. Barbara was about five foot six. Her hair was dark blond and done up in a twist. Her eyes were dark brown and twinkled with intelligence and humor. After the class Barbara and Charlie Brown walked over to where I was sitting next to another guy about my age.

"So does your wife drag you to these things too?" the guy asked. Barbara had a slightly nonplussed look on her face.

"Actually, she's not my wife," I said. "But that's an interesting idea."

I walked Barbara and her dog back to her apartment. I was very attracted to this gal, and I knew she had suggested I accompany her to her dog's training session. Still, I had no clue where things might be heading. She was, as far as I knew, practically engaged to the son of one of the Boston Brahmin families, and my forty-nine-dollar-a-week salary had grown to only sixty dollars over the past nine months. But nothing ventured, nothing gained. So as we reached the door to her apartment I said, "Would you like to go out to dinner and then a movie? Maybe tomorrow night?"

"Yes. I would. What time?" she replied.

We settled on the time, and she turned the key in her door. "I'd invite you in," she said, "but Cindy's here, and it's getting late."

"Right," I said. "I'll see you tomorrow night?"

"Can't wait." She said.

I had acquired a Vespa motor scooter for getting around Boston, and so the following evening I arrived at the front of Barbara's apartment building on Massachusetts Avenue with my Vespa. I parked it between two cars, removed my crutches from their wire coat hanger rack, and swung myself onto the sidewalk. She buzzed me into the front door. I hobbled up the four steps to the lobby area, up the elevator to her floor, down the hall to her door, and knocked. I had dressed in a coat and tie. Barbara opened the door.

"Hi. Come in," she said. I followed her down the hall to her living room. "What's it like outside? Do I need a coat?"

"Well. That depends," I responded. "How do you want to go? Do you want to take a taxi or shall we go on my Vespa?"

"Your Vespa?"

"Yes." It was a stupid question. How could she ride on my Vespa while wearing that tight skirt? I imagined that her Boston Brahmin boyfriend must take her everywhere in a taxi or what probably was his Cadillac.

"Your Vespa will be fine," she said.

I tried to hide my amazement as I said, "Then you'll probably want a coat. It's a bit chilly when we're moving."

"Fine. I'll be right back."

A few minutes later I started up my Vespa then straddled the seat. Barbara climbed on behind me sitting side saddle. She put her arms around my waste and her chin rested on my right shoulder. Her perfume smelled wonderful. I felt her breath in my right ear as she pulled herself close. We drove off. I was, at this moment, convinced that the most attractive woman I had ever met was clutching onto me for dear life.

We had dinner at a Near Eastern restaurant in Chinatown. Then we hopped back on the Vespa and drove to the movie theater.

We had probably sat through the first forty-five minutes of the movie when I turned my head in her direction, and she looked at me. I reached over with my right hand, put it behind her neck, and pulled her to me. She came very willingly. We kissed. We seemed unable to control ourselves. Finally, we parted breathlessly and decided to leave.

We went back to Barbara's apartment. She practically dragged me in the door. I hobbled behind her as we headed for the living room where we found her roommate, Cindy, in her nightgown and bathrobe with her feet up on the couch and her hair in curlers.

"Oh, hi." Cindy said. "I didn't expect you back so soon. How was the movie?"

"Uh … oh it was good," I said.

Barbara and I stood in front of Cindy holding hands. But it was clear that Cindy was in for the night.

"I guess I'd better get going," I said to Barbara. She walked me to the door. As she opened it I said, "When can we get together again?"

"Call me tomorrow," she said. Then she gave me a long, delicious kiss.

◆   ◆   ◆

On our third date, Barbara had me over to her apartment for dinner. Over our food I told her about an experience one of my fellow reporters said he had in nearby Concord, Massachusetts. He wanted to take a tour of The Old Manse, a Federal Style building located at the edge of the field you walked through to get to the bridge where the Battle of Concord had been fought. Before the tour, he strolled down to the bridge. When he looked back at the building he saw a woman with a baby in her arms standing in a second-floor window looking in his direction.

Later, when the tour arrived at the upstairs room where the woman and baby had been, he saw that it was roped off. Next to the window was a four-poster bed, and next to the bed was a cradle. He asked if there was a young woman and a baby somewhere in residence. He was told that there was not.

At the Concord Library he discovered that a young minister, his wife, and their baby had resided in the building on the day of the Battle of Concord. The minister was a Minuteman so he went off to battle. His wife, presumably, had watched him go while holding the baby in her arms. The minister never returned.

Barbara's eyes were wide open as I finished telling the story.

"Do you want to check it out?" I asked.

"You mean now?" she replied.

"Yeah. It'll be fun. Who knows? Maybe we'll see something."

Some forty-five minutes later we arrived in Concord. We putted slowly through the town center. It was very dark. I could feel the hair on the back of my neck stand up. My headlight was the only light around as I turned onto the drive at the entrance to the Old Manse. I stopped. The engine putted quietly. The headlight lit up the path, which was approximately seventy-five feet long. All was very quiet, and it was very dark outside the headlight beam.

Barbara tightened her grip on me a bit as she looked at the second story. "What's that? In that window just over the front door?" she asked.

I could see a glow in the window. It was like candlelight. "I don't know. What do you think it is?"

"I don't know. But it's really spooky. I've been here during the day but never at night. It's so dark."

"Yeah. It is." I suspected that the light in the window was a reflection from my headlight. But I said, "Wanna stop and walk around? Check it out?"

She squeezed me hard and said, "No. I don't think that's such a good idea."

I loved having Barbara this close to me, but I had to ask, "Do you want to head back?"

"Yes. Please."

"Okay."

Barbara got off the scooter, and I pushed it back with my right foot. She got back on, and we sped back the ten miles to Boston at a full 35 mph.

It was very late when we got back. We knew Cindy was in bed. Besides we had to get up for work in the morning. So, we lingered over a long kiss at her front door. Then I headed back home.

◆   ◆   ◆

On our fourth date, Barbara had me over for dinner again. It was the Wednesday night before Thanksgiving. We sat across from each other as we started to dig in. I ate one bite. It was delicious. I chewed slowly as I gazed at Barbara across the table. We both put our forks down and stared at each other as we finished chewing.

"I guess this is it," I said.

"I guess it is," she responded.

I twirled my fork on the plate. "This meal is delicious, but I don't think I can eat anymore right now."

"Me neither," she said.

She got up and left the kitchen. I followed her into her bedroom. "Cindy's with her mother out in Greenfield for the holiday weekend," she said as she turned to me at the edge of her bed. She lifted her arms around my neck and pulled me to her. I put my arms around her. Slowly we leaned over and fell onto her bed. I simply could not believe my lucky stars. This was in every way the most wonderfully beautiful, feminine woman I could ever hope to know.

Suddenly, I pulled my lips away from her. I looked at her closed eyes. She opened them and looked at me questioningly.

"Barbara Wemyss, will you marry me?"

I couldn't believe I had uttered the words. We hardly knew each other, but it felt so right.

Her lips were parted. They were very moist. Her eyes widened. Then a smile broke out on her face. "Yes, I will marry you," she said.

I kissed her very gently, almost chastely. "I do love you Barbara Wemyss. I can't believe how fast this has happened, but I do love you. I could not ask for a more wonderful woman to come into my life. Not ever."

"And I love you, Bob Ellis. I can't explain it either. I've been aware of you over the past few months, but I never would have guessed I'd be with you here like this. Yes, Robert Y. Ellis, I will marry you."

As far as I knew, Barbara still was dating her Boston Brahmin boyfriend. So she would have to break off that relationship. But that was of no concern to me at this instant.

◆   ◆   ◆

On Friday, Barbara invited me to come out to Rockport to meet her parents who were almost overwhelmingly cordial to me. Barbara's mother served lunch. Then Barbara and I headed off on my Vespa for a tour of the town of Rockport. She introduced me to Bearskin Neck, a small peninsula that formed one side of the outer and inner harbors of Rockport. It was filled with quaint shacks formerly for fishermen that had been converted into gift shops and dwellings. The harbors were dotted with small commercial fishing trawlers and lobster boats. Most of the pleasure craft had been hauled out of the water for winter storage.

We drove along the coastline in and out of various coves. We stopped at a couple of mostly deserted beaches where gulls swooped by as we strolled hand in hand at the edge of the water. This was the most peaceful spot I could imagine; it was so different from the hustle and bustle of New York's harbor and the Hudson River.

Then we returned to her parents' property. They owned and operated the Yankee Clipper Inn. It consisted of two oceanfront properties and a third building that sat across the street. Barbara showed me around the property. All the rooms were very elegant. Many had spectacular views of the Atlantic Ocean. It was a bit overwhelming for me, but over dinner, Barbara's parents made me feel as though I fit in completely.

◆　　◆　　◆

As soon as I got back from work on Monday, I telephoned my parents and told them the news. We agreed that I should bring Barbara down to Yonkers. Barbara's father had a friend in the diamond business in downtown Manhattan. The friend said he would be happy to help us find an engagement ring. So we made plans for the trip.

We borrowed one of Barbara's father's cars, and on Saturday, around noon, we pulled into my parents' driveway at 9 Elinor Place, Yonkers, N.Y.

As we entered the front door my mother met us. She stood for a few seconds and looked at the two of us. Then she grabbed Barbara's hands, and said, "Hello, dear. I'm so happy to meet you." Mom gave Barbara a light kiss on the cheek and said, "Come on up. I thought you'd be arriving about now. You're probably hungry. I have some sandwiches ready."

We followed her up the stairs as she continued to talk. "I've made the guest room ready for you, dear," she said to Barbara. "And you can sleep on the second bed in your father's room," she said to me.

She and my father used to have their bedroom on this second floor, which also had a dining room, a living room, and a kitchen. I was surprised to find that my father had moved upstairs into what used to be my room on the third floor, leaving my mother downstairs. He had moved, Mother said, because their schedules were so different.

Immediately after lunch, we drove over to Broadway, to the Henry Hudson Parkway, and down to 158th Street, where we exited. We then drove up to Amsterdam Avenue and turned right. We were in the middle of Harlem.

"There it is," I said as I pointed and slowly turned right. I drove past the Broadway Carpet Service storefront at 1968 Amsterdam Avenue, turned right on 157th Street, and found a parking space.

My father and uncle had located their business here in 1934—the year I was born. At the time, it had been an almost totally Jewish, white neighborhood. Today it was an almost totally black neighborhood. I had practically grown up here. I knew most of the merchants and many of the residents. In my earlier years, my cousins and I had played here.

Barbara's father was from Brooklyn. She had visited her grandparents in their quite elegant apartment a number of times when she was a little girl. She also had gone to Daycroft School in Stamford, Connecticut, and had made a number of excursions to the theater and opera in New York City. This was a rather different New York City.

We entered the store. The front area consisted of a long, narrow space lined with rolls of linoleum standing on end. We walked the fifty-foot length of the store to the office where my father, my uncle, and Eleanor Harris, their secretary, rose from their desks.

"Dad, Uncle Leroy, Eleanor, I want to introduce you to my fiancée, Barbara Wemyss."

They greeted us warmly.

I showed Barbara around the factory and introduced her to the guys, all of whom lived in the neighborhood and with whom I had worked several summers while in college. They greeted her very cordially and congratulated both of us. As we headed back toward the office Barbara commented, "They really are nice people, aren't they?"

"Yes they are," I said. "I've known them for years. Some of them have known me since I was very little. In a way, I feel like I was raised here."

We went back to the office. "We need to get going," I said to everyone. "We're expected downtown."

"I'll see you to the door," my father said. We started toward the front door. "I wanted to give this to you," he said as he handed me an envelope.

I opened the envelope and found three hundred-dollar bills.

"My God, Dad!"

"I don't know if it will be enough," he said, "but your mother and I wanted to help with the engagement ring."

I showed it to Barbara. "Oh my," she said. "Thank you, Mr. Ellis. That's so kind of you."

"Well, you'd better get going before you run out of time," he said.

"Okay. Thanks, Dad."

"This is amazing," I said to Barbara as we left the store. "I can't believe my father gave us this money."

"Why not?" Barbara asked.

"He and I have been sort of estranged ever since I went to Boston. He wasn't happy that I went to work for the *Monitor*. And somehow I think he's unhappy that I have followed the path that I have. He expected me to do great things for civil liberties as a lawyer. And now he hands me this envelope. How do you explain it?"

"Perhaps it's because he loves you."

◆   ◆   ◆

Mary Baker Eddy made no provision for weddings in her churches. And so, three months later, on a cold, dreary, snowy March 4, 1961, we were married in the Congregational Church in Rockport. I no longer was wearing a cast, and I was able to shed my cane long enough to walk down the aisle. The service was conducted by Rev. Ed Nutting, a Congregational minister, but many of the words and music that made up the service came out of *Science and Health* and the *Christian Science Hymnal.*

Immediately after the ceremony, Barbara and I dashed through the scattered snowflakes and down the long path to the street where my father-in-law's Cadillac awaited us. Five minutes later, we arrived at the Yankee Clipper Inn for the reception.

Barbara and I were at the mercy of the photographer and had little chance to take part in the celebration. All we got to eat was a bite of the wedding cake, which we each had to consume for the photographer. Later, people would remark what a scandal it was that we couldn't enjoy our own party. But I had to admit that I was in such a fog of wedding bliss that none of it registered with me.

Later, Barbara and I headed to our new apartment in Boston for our wedding night. The following day, we drove to the Poconos in Pennsylvania for our week of connubial bliss at Strickland's—a huge honeymoon hotel.

"It really is something the way everything has worked out," I said as we pulled away from the reception.

"And so fast!" Barbara responded. "You know, my mother's afraid it might not last, but she and Dad are very fond of you."

"Yeah. They've made that very clear. And my mom's thrilled with you. I'm sure you know that."

"Yes. She's made that abundantly clear. I'm not so sure about your father, though. Don't get me wrong. He was very nice this weekend, but I sensed that he wasn't comfortable. It was almost like he didn't approve."

It was true that my father had seemed a little stiff at times. To some extent I believed he simply wasn't used to the gregarious, hail-fellow-well-met, generous atmosphere my father-in-law projected. But I also suspected that Christian Science was at the bottom of it. Barbara's parents and most of their friends were Christian Scientists, and I was unabashedly committed to Christian Science.

Then there were the politics. My in-laws were staunch Republicans and avid anticommunists. They agreed halfheartedly that McCarthy "probably" had gone too far. My father on the other hand had gone to the Supreme Court over the McCarthy threat! He stayed silent on the issue, but I suspected he had a hard time containing himself.

"You could be right," I said. "But you know what? Right now I just want to be with you and enjoy the moment." I looked at her; she returned my gaze with a very inviting smile, took my right hand, and squeezed.

RAIN

In the fall of 1964 Dana Gatlin, approached me. He now was a sports writer and I was a staff writer for the City Desk at the *Monitor*.

"Would you ever be interested in leaving the *Monitor*?" he asked.

"What do you mean?" The thought had never occurred to me.

"Well," Dana said, "I've been covering the National Figure Skating Championships at the Boston Skating Club, and one of the members of their executive board approached me. Seems they're looking for someone to run their Central Office here in Boston—someone with writing experience as well as people skills. I have no idea why, but your name popped into my head. So I thought I'd ask you."

I had been aware that Dana was covering the national championships. They were in the headlines of all the Boston dailies, but I had not paid much attention to them.

"I have no idea. It's never crossed my mind," I said.

"Would you mind if I gave them your name?'

I could not imagine why my name might have popped into Dana's head. Was this Divine Intelligence at work?

"Well, I suppose there's no harm in my talking with them," I said.

Five months later, after many interviews, negotiations, and much soul-searching that left me believing Divine Intelligence was indeed leading me, I left the *Monitor* and became business manager of the United States Figure Skating Association. I worked in their central office in Copley Square in Boston. A substantial increase in salary made it possible for Barbara and me to purchase our first home in North Reading, about a half hour train ride from Boston.

A year went by before my parents finally came up from New York to see our new home. We had invited them many times. Each time, though, there was some reason why my father could not make the trip. Barbara said it was because he didn't want to see us.

Finally, very late on a Saturday evening in early March, they arrived in the pouring rain.

"We were getting worried about you," I said as I followed them through our front door.

"It's just that Daddy didn't seem to be able to get away from the factory," my mother said. "We're so sorry."

"Well, we better get you all settled. Once you freshen up we can have dinner," I said.

As soon as my parents came back downstairs we sat down to dinner. Barbara had cooked one of my father's favorites—Yankee pot roast.

"This really is good, Honey," I said.

"Yes it is," my mother agreed. "And your table is lovely. Isn't it attractive James?"

Dad didn't answer.

"James? Isn't it attractive?"

"Uh ... yes. I suppose it is."

"So how long are you going to be able to stay? Barbara and I have taken tomorrow off so we can be with you," I said.

"Taken off?" Dad asked. "Do you work on Sunday?"

"No. I meant from church."

"He means he's gotten someone to substitute for him. You know he's the First Reader, James," Mother explained.

"Oh. Yes. And you, Barbara? Are you expected there, too?" my father asked.

"Well, I usually usher, but I've told them that I can't be there tomorrow."

My father looked at me, "Tell me about your work with the figure skaters."

"Well, uh, let me see. You know the U.S. Figure Skating Association controls amateur figure skating in the United States—"

"Why did they hire you?" he interrupted.

"Because I was a staff writer on the *Monitor*, and they wanted someone with experience in writing for their monthly magazine. They also thought I could get things better organized in the overall office."

"What about the law?"

"I don't know how to answer that, except to say it evidently wasn't meant to be."

"What's that supposed to mean? You spent three years studying for the law," he said.

"The only thing I can tell you is that I'm where I am now, and we're very happy."

Dad displayed no emotion. His eyes went to Barbara; then to my mother. Finally, his eyes moved to somewhere halfway up the wall behind my mother.

Mother said, "Oh, James, won't you please relax?"

"I am perfectly relaxed," he replied.

"No you're not. You're as tight as a drum. Barbara's cooked us a lovely dinner, and we're not able to enjoy it. Bob and Barbara have started a lovely home, and we should be enjoying it with them. They need to know we are happy for them."

"Happy?" my father declared now looking up at the ceiling. "Is that what I should be? I should be *happy*?" His hands rested on either side of his plate. "I wonder how I might manage that?" he said sarcastically with a wry grin.

"Oh, James. Let's not get into this now. This isn't the place or the time,"

"Oh? Not the place or time? Well why not? I'd say it's time they knew."

"Please, James!" my mother pleaded.

"Please what?" Dad shouted. "What do you want from me?" His face had turned beet red. He leaped out of his chair practically overturning it, and walked to the center of the room and stood with his back to us.

"I'll clear the table," Barbara finally said.

"Clearing the table is not going to help," my father said in very measured tones. You could tell his words were coming through clenched teeth. "I'm leaving!"

"What?" I exclaimed. I looked to my mother.

"Oh, James, you can't mean that," she said, as she started to get up from the table.

"Oh, can't I?" he replied. "Just watch me!" He headed for the coat closet.

"Dad! Wait!" I shouted as we got up. "Look outside. It's pouring rain and dark. Where will you go? You can't just leave. What about Mom?"

"I'll take the train. Katherine can have the car."

"The train? There won't be any train until tomorrow."

"I don't care. I can't stay here. You can drive me to the train station and leave me there." He grabbed his coat and headed out the door.

I turned to my mother. "What should we do?"

"You'd better follow him out to your car."

"What if he insists on my driving him to the train?"

"Then drive him to the train. He can't go anywhere if there are no trains. Let's let Divine Mind govern us. We'll work to know that there is a solution even though we can't see it. What you don't know is that this isn't the first time he's blown up at me."

"This has happened before?"

"Yes. It's been going on for a number of years. It's a long story. You'd better go to your father," Mom said

When Barbara and I had first driven to Yonkers, and Mother had told me that my father had moved upstairs, I had guessed something was not right between them. But this revelation came as a shock.

"Jesus," I said as I grabbed my jacket, and ran through the pouring rain to our car. Dad sat on the passenger side looking through the steamy windshield into the dark, pouring rain. I put my hands on the steering wheel, closed my eyes, and silently asked God what to do. "Are you sure you want to do this, Dad?" I heard myself ask.

"Yes."

"But you have no clothes with you, no toiletries. How about money?"

"I have money in my pocket. I'll be fine as long as I'm not here."

"But, Dad—"

"Don't argue with me, Bob," he interrupted. "Just take me to the station."

I said nothing more, started the engine, wiped the windshield on the inside with my forearm, backed out of the driveway, and drove toward the railroad station in Reading. The rain was coming down very hard. I put the windshield wipers on high, but I still had to proceed slowly.

"What am I going to do?" I kept asking myself. "This doesn't make any sense. He won't be able to go anywhere if I drop him off. He'll have to sit alone in his wet clothes all night. There's no building for him to stay in. There's just a roof. How can I leave him waiting there overnight? What will happen to him? Dear God, tell me what to do."

I pulled into the parking lot and turned off the headlights and engine. Lightning suddenly flashed, showing for one brief second the entire railroad station with its empty tracks and parking lot. Thunder roared a second later; it was very close. Ours was the only car in the parking lot.

"I can't leave you here," I shouted over the din from the rain. "I can't do it."

"Well, you'll just have to," my father shouted back.

"But, Dad, what will you do? Where will you go?"

"I don't know," he shouted. "All I know is that I am not going back there."

We both were talking to the waterfall of rain pouring over the windshield. How could he even think of stepping out into that downpour, running for cover, and just sitting there? "There won't be any trains until tomorrow. You can't just sit there all night."

"Bob," he returned in an angry voice, "I am not going back to that house."

Another streak of lightning. Another burst of thunder.

"I cannot leave you here. I won't do it. Please listen to me," I pleaded.

"No. You listen to me. I cannot go back there. I can't stand all the phony, sanctimonious sweetness and light any longer."

Oh God, I thought to myself. There was no way for me to respond. Not here. All I dared do was try to get him to come back to our home.

"Look. I know you're angry. I know our house is small, but we have a hide-a-bed downstairs. You won't have to sleep with Mom. Please. Let's go back. Maybe in the morning we'll be able to sort things out."

"There'll be no sorting things out this time," he said.

"All right. Maybe you're right, but at least you can sleep under a roof and out of the rain. Then head back tomorrow. Come home. I'm begging you. Please. I can't leave you here."

He said nothing.

"Look, Dad," the words were coming out automatically, as though I wasn't creating them. "Before I came out here, Mom told me that she and you have been having problems. I'm not sure what's going on between the two of you, but staying here all night isn't going to accomplish anything. I refuse to leave you here alone. And staying here will only make the both of us more miserable than we already are.

"Mmm," he grunted.

"So, now I'm pleading with you. Please let me drive you back to our house. Please! There need be no discussion when we get back. We won't try to get you to change your mind or anything, but at least I'll know you're safe in our house. Then, in the morning you can go back to New York by train if that's what you want."

We sat silently for a few seconds. Finally I asked, "So. Can I drive us back?" He continued looking at the downpour on the windshield. I stayed silent.

"I suppose you're right about not accomplishing anything by staying here," he finally responded.

"But you find it difficult to go back to our house, and so would I if I were in your shoes. But look, I promise I won't allow any discussion after we get back. All I'm asking of you is that you don't make me leave you here."

Somehow, though I wanted to, I couldn't bring myself to say "I love you." It had been so long since any display of affection had passed between us. I looked at him as he continued staring out the windshield. I suddenly realized that I felt terribly sorry for him. It was all I could do to get the words out without choking, "Dad, I can't leave you here. Please come back."

Silence.

Finally he said, "All right, but don't expect anything to change."

Before he could change his mind I started the car, turned on the lights, backed out, and headed home.

Mother and Barbara were in the living room. My father looked at my mother. "Your son can be very persuasive," was all he said. He removed his jacket, draped it over the back of a chair to dry, walked to the hide-a-bed, sat down, and leaned back with his hands on his knees.

"I've promised Dad there will be no discussion," I said. "We're just going to get some sleep and let tomorrow take care of itself."

It was approaching midnight. My father started up the stairs toward the guest room. Mother looked at me and nodded gently. She then followed Dad. Barbara and I went to our bedroom. We heard nothing else from my parents that night.

"Your mother filled me in while you were off with your father," Barbara said as we climbed into bed. "I guess he's been unhappy for a while. He's even asked her for a divorce several times. But then he seems to completely forget that he asked her. Things go back to normal for a while. Then he blows up again."

My parents had been married for almost forty years. In recent years there had been some hint that things were not quite right. Still, this revelation came out of the blue.

I said, "Christ! I had no idea. I mean, I've known for a long time that Dad always seemed to be touchy, but I've never seen anything like this. What are we going to do?"

"I don't see how there's anything we can do. This is between your parents," Barbara said.

We all rose early the next morning. The rain had stopped; some clouds moved quickly through the deep, blue sky; and the sun was shining brightly.

At breakfast we were very polite to each other. Nothing was said about last night. Soon my parents were gone. Barbara and I stared at each other.

"What the hell was that all about?" I asked. "You'd think nothing had happened."

"It is strange. Maybe they resolved things last night."

"I find that hard to believe. What I don't get is how my father could have been so angry last night, yet they appeared so calm this morning. They've been married, what, thirty-six years? In that time, Mom's gone from being a Broadway actress, before she met my father, to a busy Christian Science practitioner. And Dad has grown to resent it more and more as each year goes by. I know she's happy with her work. She's always talking about it. But Dad? He spends his days in Harlem from early morning to late at night. I could see Mom getting along fine if they were to separate. But Dad? What the hell would he do?"

"I don't know."

I realized for the first time that Sunday morning just how excluded from all us Christian Scientists my father must have felt.

HOLIDAY MAGIC

I spent the next years reorganizing the U.S. Figure Skating Association's Central Office, moving it into new quarters, redesigning the magazine, hiring staff to carry things forward. I had started as Business Manager and now was Executive Secretary.

Then, about five years into my tenure, the Executive Board told me that they wanted a "Mr. Figure Skating" to be in charge, someone who could speak for the sport like the baseball commissioner speaks for baseball. They encouraged me to take up skating, maybe get into ice dancing. But it simply wasn't in me. I really didn't find the sport all that fascinating. The work I had been doing to this point was interesting, even fun. But toward the end I could tell the board was tiring of me, and I of them. I would never be their Mr. Figure Skating.

Barbara and I prayed mightily. I was making what seemed like very good money. Where could we turn for an activity that would keep us in a similar or better earnings situation?

One evening Barbara and I had dinner with Dana and his wife Mitzi and another couple—Dave and Mary Haroldson. We were all Christian Scientists. Barbara and I described to our friends our present situation and some of the efforts we had made interviewing with head hunters and how nothing seemed to click, when Dave said, "You know, I just met a guy who lives down in Long Island. He has a fairly new business going, but he's been very successful. He's looking for someone in the Boston area to get things going here. He's a Christian Scientist. In fact, a lot of his associates are CS as well. Would you like me to give him your name?"

"What kind of business is it?" Barbara asked.

"It has to do with a whole new line of cosmetics. He showed them to us. They're quite different from anything on the market today. They're all made from natural products—like a hand cream made from avocado or a strawberry based facial cleanser. It's nice stuff. He seems to be doing quite well with it."

Barbara and I looked at each other. I said, "I never dreamed we'd look into cosmetics. On the other hand, I also never dreamed I'd get involved in figure skating. I suppose there's no harm in your giving him our name. It sounds kind of intriguing," I said. Barbara smiled and nodded.

I met with Dave's friend, Steve Mishkin, in his home on Long Island. He showed me the cosmetics. They seemed to me to be quite unusual and very appealing. I asked him how he sold them. He said that some people opened salons, gave make-up lessons, facials. But the real money, he said, was to be earned by recruiting more distributors who in turn were to recruit more distributors. Every time you recruited someone you made money. Every time someone you had recruited brought another distributor in under him, you made money. And every time anyone within your organization made a sale of cosmetics you made even more money. The more distributors you had, the more money you made.

Soon after my meeting with Steve, Barbara and I invested twenty-five hundred dollars to receive a supply of cosmetics and sales kits. We began to recruit distributors. Not many. But it looked promising. Barbara enjoyed demonstrating the products to potential customers. Three months later, I gave my notice to the USFSA. We no longer had a steady paycheck, and then everything came to a standstill. We rented an office and hired sales people to recruit more distributors. Nothing seemed to work. To tide us over I went to work for my father-in-law as a desk clerk at his newly acquired Ralph Waldo Emerson Inn in Rockport.

On Tuesday, October 14, 1968, Barbara and I sat at our kitchen table silently preparing our coffee. It was the day after the Columbus Day weekend. It was bright and sunny outside. Barbara's bathrobe was pulled up tightly around her neck to guard against the fall chill. The temperature had reached down near freezing last night, though it was warming nicely this morning. To save on fuel, we had not turned on the oil burner for the year.

I said: "Last night your father reminded me that he'll be closing the inn for the season soon. That means I'll be out of a job, and I don't know what the hell we're going to do for money. I don't know how we let ourselves get sucked into Holiday Magic. We're getting nowhere. So, I'm going to see Bill Downing this afternoon." Bill was our Christian Science practitioner.

"What do you propose to tell him?"

I looked down into my coffee. "I don't know for sure. It's just that I'm feeling so confused right now, even panicky."

Barbara's brown eyes became wide as saucers. "I've been worried, too, but I was afraid to say anything. You've been so hell-bent to go for this program."

"I know. But I have to admit we're throwing good money after bad. And we can't keep it up. There's nothing left. I don't even know where our next mortgage payment's coming from. I've been worrying about it to the point now where I can't sleep."

"Have you thought about how you're going to pay Bill?"

"Yeah, I know what you mean. But he always sends us a bill. Hopefully, we'll be in a better position before we have to pay it."

Bill charged ten dollars for an office visit.

"Well, let's not give up quite yet. It's good that you're seeing Bill. I'll be interested to hear what he has to say," Barbara said.

◆   ◆   ◆

Bill Downing lived in Boston on the ninth floor of a Charles River Park highrise. As we walked through the living room to his study, I saw the sun sparkling off the river and trees showing their late fall colors with the city of Cambridge in the distance.

Piles of papers were stacked on a couch in his study. The surface of his desk was covered with the *Christian Science Monitor*, several editions of the *Christian Science Sentinel*, the *Christian Science Journal*, and other works. A typewriter stood on its own stand with paper in it that was partially filled with typing. Bill often wrote articles for the Christian Science periodicals, or he could be in the middle of a letter to one of his patients.

"It's good to see you," he said as he looked at me with his normal, gentle smile. He was about my height and slender with a full head of dark hair. He didn't have a hint of gray although I knew he was more my in-laws' age than mine. Both he and my father-in-law had served in the Second World War. He once told me of his experiences as a medic on the beach at Anzio in Italy—one of the most brutal battles of the war. He described to me how, while assisting the surgeons in the emergency operating tent, he had learned the power of relying on God. "Knowing to myself that God was with us in that tent was what got me through," He had once told me.

He went behind his desk and sat down. "So, what brings you here?"

"Let's see. You know we went into Holiday Magic?" I asked.

"No. I don't think I knew that. What's Holiday Magic?

"It's a really nice line of cosmetics." I looked at him expecting a reaction, but he maintained his expectant look. "All the items are made with natural ingredients like strawberries or avocado or papaya—all kinds of exotic flavors. You'd love their aroma."

"Sounds very nice. So have you opened a salon?"

"No. They're mainly sold through a special marketing program."

"And how does that work?"

I described the marketing program to him. Strangely, I found myself feeling the same excitement I had felt when the program was first described to me.

I saw Bill's eyes narrow a bit, and he asked, "How did you find out about this enterprise?"

I told him about the dinner during which Dave had mentioned Steve.

"Before you go on, Bob, can you describe what led you to believe this was the right occupation? Was it simply the fact that Christian Scientists introduced you to it?"

"Well, I have to say the fact that Steve is a Christian Scientist and that we met a lot of others in New York who had joined the program, was important to us. We believed that there was an element of principle involved in it. We had to believe these others had done the same kind of praying we had done before investing in this program."

"Well, I understand what you're saying. But there was something more. You wouldn't go into a business just because a Christian Scientist recommended it to you. I don't believe I'm hearing why it is you and Barbara decided to invest in this particular scheme. The fact that you like the product and the fact that a lot of Christian Scientists were involved in it doesn't tell me enough. There are many fine enterprises with many Christian Scientists involved. You didn't have to pick this one There's something else, isn't there? Something that drew you in. Can you articulate it for me?"

"Well, yeah. I have to admit it was the money. The kind of money that was discussed was incredible."

"All right then. Perhaps now you should explain why you are here."

"Well, I have to admit it's embarrassing." I took a deep breath and said, "We've completely run out of money. We've gotten so short of cash that sometimes we can buy only twenty-five cents worth of gas at a time. I'm working for my father-in-law as a desk clerk on the 3:00 to 11:00 shift, but that doesn't bring in enough money. Besides, that'll end in a month. I have no idea what we're going to do after that."

"Would you mind telling me why you think things have come to this?"

I took a deep breath and let out a huge sigh. "I honestly am so confused over this. I just can't understand how we could have gone so wrong. We thought we were doing the right thing. We thought we were led to go into this, and look what it's brought us."

"Let me ask you a question, Bob. You've described an interesting marketing scheme. And you've told me of your motivation, which was to make what you called 'incredible' amounts of money. So ultimately, what is it that you are selling?"

"Yeah. I get it. It's making money. That's what we're selling," I said.

"Making money that you call *incredible*," Bill said. His eyebrows were considerably higher than normal. His eyes bore into mine. "All right, I believe we've gotten to the root of the problem, and it's time we started handling it scientifically. First, I don't believe your problem is one of not having enough income or not knowing where to go from here—whether to leave Holiday Magic and whether to seek another job."

"You don't?"

"No, I don't. This goes much deeper than that. Just before you arrived here I was reading an article in the *Journal* that I feel applies directly to your problem. It's called "Handling Animal Magnetism in Healing.""

"Animal magnetism? I handle animal magnetism every day."[1]

"I'm sure you do. But I'd like to ask you, how do you define animal magnetism?"

"Well, Mrs. Eddy calls it the 'specific term for error' I believe. She also says it is 'mortal mind.' What she means is that it's all the wrong thinking that's going on."

"What wrong thinking? On whose part?" Bill asked

"On the part of everyone who is thinking incorrectly."

"In other words, most of humanity?"

"Well, yes," I said.

"Anything else?"

"She also calls it 'hypnotism.' I've often thought of it as a material belief that becomes so prevalent we find ourselves being mesmerized or hypnotized by it. Like all the ads on TV telling us everybody's going to get a cold so we should buy

---

1.   Animal magnetism is, to Christian Scientists, an extremely important subject. The dictionary definition only gives a hint as to how Christian Scientists use the term. *Science and Health* says, "As named in Christian Science, animal magnetism or hypnotism is the specific term for error, or mortal mind. It is the false belief that mind is in matter." Animal magnetism, then, is *an all-inclusive term* for any mortal mind suggestion that opposes the understanding in Christian Science that there is no matter, that all is spiritual. Christian Scientists are admonished to mentally deny the existence of animal magnetism every day

cold medicine. Next thing you know, we've convinced ourselves that we are going to get a cold."

I saw in his expression that it was time for me to connect the dots.

"So you're telling me that Barbara and I were mesmerized by the Holiday Magic pitch?" I asked.

"I'm not telling you anything. That's not my job. Here's my point. The underlying error behind every case that any practitioner has to handle is *the basic belief that matter is real*. If we only handle the claim of disease itself and/or its symptoms … we are merely handling the *effects* of the basic error, leaving the *centuries-old underlying belief in matter and all things material* untouched."

I was pretty sure I knew what he was getting at. But I hated to admit it. Suddenly, though, I heard myself saying, "One word keeps coming to me. I'm not sure why, but it popped into my head a couple of minutes ago."

"And what is that?" Bill asked.

"Avarice. I'm not even sure I know what it means."

"Hmm. Very interesting. Let's look it up," He reached for his dictionary, which was open on a corner of his desk. "Let's see now. Here are some synonyms, 'greed, covetousness, cupidity.' How about this one: 'materialism?'" He looked up at me.

"Yeah. I see what you mean. So you're saying we've let ourselves get mesmerized by a materialistic scheme. Holiday Magic is a scheme for achieving material aims."

"I'm not saying anything about Holiday Magic," Bill said. "For all I know, Holiday Magic cosmetics are the most wonderful product since sliced bread. What we have to do here is examine *your thinking process*. We need to know that you are not a child of human avarice—your word—rather you are a child of God, of Divine Mind, Divine Intelligence. We need to know that no mortal mind belief *that matter is real* can have any effect on you whatsoever. That's the basic error."

"I hate to admit it," I said, "but it does seem that we've allowed ourselves to get caught up in a materialistic get-rich-quick scheme. So it would seem that we ought to quit Holiday Magic."

"That has to be your decision. You know a practitioner never gives advice,"

"So what do we do now?" I asked.

"What *we* do is the only thing *we* can do. We work to know that no animal magnetism suggestion that matter is real can have any influence on you and yours. We work to know that there is only one infinite Mind and its creation. It's such a basic truth that I often wonder why it is so hard for us to grasp it. Mind being infinite there is no room for anything else. Any suggestion to the contrary is nothing more than error, a mistake. We need to erase it. We need to eliminate it from our calculations. If you make a mistake in mathematics you don't leave it and continue your calculations. You erase it, and then go on with your calculations. That's what has to happen here. You need to get back to the basics and let only Divine Intelligence enter your consciousness. Rest in the fact that only God, Divine Mind, Divine Love, Divine Principle is operating. Always remember, Bob, whatever answers you need exist now. At this very instant, infinite Divine Mind knows."

As always at the end of a session, Bill would bring me back to where I should have been—resting in a sense of God's infinite presence. Nothing had changed, of course. We still were faced with what seemed to be insurmountable debt and total failure with Holiday Magic. I had no idea what our answers would be. But the operative word was "seemed." Regardless of what seemed to be our situation, answers did exist. Right at that instant. I had only to let Divine Intelligence operate in my consciousness, and the answers would appear.

Finally he said, "I think this would be a good place for us to stop. Would you agree?"

"Yes, I would," I said as I looked at my watch. It was just after two o'clock—time for me to leave. I got up, reached across his desk, and shook his hand. "Thanks, Bill. I really mean it. I feel a lot better. I know we're going to get our answer."

He walked me to the front door. As I walked down the hall to the elevator I felt as though I was walking on air. All sense of material concern had been lifted from my shoulders. It had been a long time since I felt that I had been in touch with God. I sensed his presence—a feeling of spiritual peace. I felt I could let go of all mortal mind thinking, and let Divine Intelligence operate. This was something I knew I had not done for some time.

Soon I was back in my car and heading toward Rockport for my shift at the front desk of the Emerson Inn. "Okay," I said to myself. "I'm going to rest in what Bill said and in the work he is doing for me. I'm going to do my best not to allow any mortal mind suggestion into my consciousness. I'm going to stop thinking about all this money stuff, and just listen for God's thoughts, nothing else."

I spent eight busy hours at the front desk managing, for the most part, to dismiss any temptation to ruminate over our problems. "No," I kept saying to myself. "I'm only going to let God's thoughts in."

In the middle of my shift I had dinner with my in-laws in the hotel's elegant dining room. "It's good to see you looking more like yourself," my father-in-law said.

"I had a session with Bill just before I came here." Normally I would not have told them anything. But this seemed to be a good time to let them know what Barbara and I were going through. "We've gotten ourselves into a pickle. I wanted to get Bill's help."

"What sort of pickle?" Dad responded.

"Well, truth be told, we're just about broke." There. I had said it. I hated having to admit it to my in-laws. Dad had shown his skepticism early on when we had told him about Holiday Magic. To his credit, he had remained silent ever since.

"Oh dear," my mother-in-law said.

"Yeah. Well, I know we're going to figure things out. Bill was a real help to me. I've not been thinking things through as scientifically as I should have. I can see that. I don't know what the answer is going to be, but I know we'll be okay."

"Well. Good," Dad said. And he dropped the subject.

At 11:00 PM, the end of my shift, I climbed into my car to begin my drive back home. I had nothing to hold my attention other than the white line in the middle of the road. In spite of our near destitute situation, my belief in Christian Science still was total. Even so, I had a hard time not wondering, "What the hell are we going to do?"

HOME

The next morning at breakfast I described my visit with Bill to Barbara.

"You know," she said. "I had a thought come to me while you were with Bill. I kind of dismissed it, but now I'm not so sure. It occurred to me that maybe if we sold our house we could make enough money to pay off our debts and start afresh."

"Sell our house?" I was stunned. "Where would we live?"

"I don't know. But I have to admit that I've been wondering if Holiday Magic was a mistake." She paused then said, "By the way, your mother called yesterday."

"Oh yeah? What'd she want?" I asked.

"She said she simply felt impelled to call. I told her you were seeing Bill."

"Did you tell her why?"

"I told her we were hopelessly broke."

"Jesus! What'd she say?"

"She said she would work to know[1] that, no matter what mortal mind might be suggesting to us at the moment, the answers to our problems exist right now."

"Kind of amazing isn't it? I mean all this coming to you and my mother at the same time I was with Bill?" I paused for a moment then said, "I also told your parents."

"You did? What did they say?"

"Nothing, really. Your father was glad I had gone to see Bill."

Barbara stayed silent for a moment, then said, "Well, here's what I'm going to do. I'm going to get dressed, head over to Reading Realty, and see if they can tell us what we could get for our house." She stared at me almost defiantly, daring me to say, "Don't."

I said nothing for a spell. Then suddenly I felt a weight lift off my shoulders, and I said, "You know, I got nowhere yesterday with my readings for tonight. I

---

1.   The phrase "work to know" means that the individual is seeking the spiritual under-
     standing one needs regarding any given situation.

couldn't get any sense of what the subject should be. But it's just come to me. I'm going to look up everything I can find on the subject of 'home.'"

"Home?"

"Yes. Think about it. This house is our home, and we're thinking of selling it. Where will our next home be?"

◆   ◆   ◆

As with Sunday services, Wednesday evening meetings include a sermon made up exclusively of citations from the *Bible* and *Science and Health*. However, whereas the citations for Sunday are worked out by a committee at the Mother Church, the Wednesday citations have to be worked out each week by the First Reader—myself in this case.

I went directly to my study, pulled out my concordances to the Bible and to *Science and Health,* and started looking for anything I could find on the subject of "home."

There were fifty citations in the Old and New Testaments and fifty in *Science and Health*. But my finger went immediately to 1 Corinthians 5:1–8, "For we know that if our earthly house of this tabernacle were dissolved, we have a building of God, an house not made with hands, eternal in the heavens. For in this we groan, earnestly desiring to be clothed upon with our house which is from heaven: … Therefore we are always confident, knowing that, whilst we are at home in the body, we are absent from the Lord: … We are confident, I say, and willing rather to be absent from the body, and to be present with the Lord."

This, I thought, would be a good beginning for the Bible section, which should last about six or seven minutes. Then I thought of the story of Ruth in the Old Testament and her willingness to leave her homeland and travel with her mother-in-law to a new homeland in Bethlehem. As long as she could be with the God of Israel, she cared not where her physical home was. She was blessed many times once she made that decision.

Then I thought of the Twenty-third Psalm and David's words, "I will dwell in the house of the Lord forever." I knew that in *Science and Health*, Mrs. Eddy defined the word "house" as "consciousness." And she took the synonym, Love, for the word, Lord. So the verse reads, "I will dwell in the consciousness of Love forever."

Then I searched for citations from *Science and Health*. Finally, I went to work sorting out all the citations I had found and putting them into a logical order so that they would read smoothly. I ended up with only the three citations from the

Bible, starting with First Corinthians, then the story of Ruth, and I ended with the Twenty-third Psalm, one of my favorites—especially the way it reads in the King James Version.

Next, I sorted the citations from *Science and Health* starting with Mrs. Eddy's statement, "Home is the dearest spot on earth, and it should be the centre, though not the boundary, of the affections."[2] Then I worked through those quotes that described home as heaven and house as consciousness of Love. I ended my readings with, "Pilgrim on earth thy home is heaven; stranger, thou art the guest of God."[3]

When I finished, I leaned back in my chair and remained quiet for a spell. Sometimes working out a sermon was a struggle for me. Inspiration seemed hard to come by. But every now and then, I would feel myself filled with inspiration, and the preparation would seem effortless. This was one of those times. I knew, deep down in my heart, that God did speak to us if we would only listen. I had said to Barbara that it had "come to me" to work these readings around the subject of home. I knew at this instant that the subject of "home" had come to me from God. And I knew at this instant that, no matter what the material suggestions might be, our true home was with God—right now. Right here.

This kind of thinking was a part of me. Frequently I would experience it while studying. But it also could occur while I was commuting on the train to Boston or while waiting for an appointment. This thinking took place anywhere I might find myself alone. I would take advantage of those moments for contemplating my relationship with God. I supposed it was what some people might call a form of meditation. All my surroundings would become unimportant; they would almost vanish. All would be very peaceful and very quiet.

I was startled out of my reverie when the phone rang. It was my mother, "Hello, dear," she said. "How are you?"

"I'm doing very well," I said. "I just finished working out tonight's readings."

"What's your subject? Do you mind telling me?"

"It's 'home.'"

"Isn't that interesting," she said. "That's why I'm calling you, in a way. I spoke to Daddy last night. You know Barbara and I spoke yesterday? I told him what Barbara had said, and he immediately responded that there would be a place for you at the factory."

"You're kidding."

---

2.   *S&H* 58:21
3.   *S&H* 254:31

"No, dear. I'm not. He was quite serious."

"I don't know what to say. The idea's never crossed my mind."

"I can understand that. And it's not something you even have to consider."

"I can't imagine what Barbara's reaction will be. But at least it's good to know there's an option available to us if we leave here."

"Well, I'll let you get back to your work."

"Okay, Mother, and thank you. I really appreciate the call. We love you."

"I know you do, dear," she said. "Bye, bye."

We hung up. I was stunned. Dad and I were estranged. There was no denying it. Especially since that rainy weekend. And yet he was my father. I was extremely conflicted over our relationship. I loved him. I cherished my childhood memories with him. I had to believe that he loved me, in spite of his disappointment in me. I was not disappointed in myself in spite of our present situation. I knew that I had been led to follow the path I presently was treading. I had no idea where Barbara and I might be headed. But, after my experience with working out tonight's readings, I was certain that we would know soon enough.

◆　　　◆　　　◆

Six weeks later I headed out the front door of our house with my hands full of two suitcases. I had another two smaller cases under my arms.

"Well, I guess this is it," I said as Barbara followed me down the steps to our driveway.

"I guess so," she replied, "although I still can't believe it's come to this."

During the past weeks we had put our house on the market, but it hadn't yet sold. We hoped to get $16,995 for it. We had paid $13,500 for it five years earlier. The $3,500 profit, plus about $1,500 in equity, minus expenses, would make it possible to pay off all our debts and have a little leftover. I also had resigned my position as First Reader at church. That was hard. I hated to leave in the middle of my three-year term.

I put my suitcases in the car, and turned to my wife and said,. "Well, here goes."

"I love you, Bob."

"And I love you. More than anything."

"Everything is going to work out. Isn't it?"

"It has to. We'll be okay. We just have to keep knowing everything will work out for us." We wrapped our arms around each other and hugged for a long time.

"You drive carefully," she said after a moment. "And call me when you get to Yonkers. Let me know you're okay."

◆   ◆   ◆

Within a month Barbara followed me to New York. We moved our belongings out of our North Reading home into an apartment just four house fronts up 263rd Street from the home where I had been raised while at PS 81. It seemed a bit unsettling to find myself returning to the old neighborhood. Barbara and I went to work at Broadway Carpet. We had arrived just as the Christmas shopping season was starting. Folks bought a lot of linoleum and carpet to spruce up for the holidays. But after the Christmas rush Barbara found a job in the Times Square area working for a large fashion house.

I waited on customers in the store and made calls in homes all over the city. After selling some family an apartment full of carpet, I would be in charge of making sure things were done the way the customer wanted. But when we got on the job, Eldred Salmon, who had been with Broadway Carpet for years and was in charge of installations, told me what to do. I'd get things for him and hammer down tackless stripping the way he instructed. It was an interesting, nice relationship.

But the business had been founded on a city-wide habit of removing your wool rugs from your apartment in the spring, putting down a hemp or sisal rug for coolness in the summer, then returning the wool rug for warmth as the next winter approached. Broadway Carpet picked up thousands of rugs each spring, cleaned and stored them until delivery in the fall. By the time Barbara and I arrived on the scene, however, window air conditioners had been invented. As well, more and more people were installing wall-to-wall carpet. So not nearly as many rugs were coming in for cleaning each year. The factory, which had once been a movie theater, was becoming quiet. The hundreds of shelves, which used to be packed with cleaned, wrapped rugs, were less and less full. When I had worked here in summers while in college, this place had been a very busy, exhausting place to work. Now, it was rather still.

What were we to do? My father, uncle, and I finally agreed that we should shut down the cleaning plant and farm out the business to another more efficient plant. We still picked up and delivered the rugs. But suddenly, the entire carpet cleaning section of the building went quiet. There was no more carpet-beating machine, no more wash floor, no more huge ringer, and no more dry-room. The machines were there. But now they only collected dust.

Sales of new goods also were not showing any sign of growth, possibly reflecting a change in the neighborhood. The drug scene, which was most prevalent down around 125th Street, was working its way north—toward us.

◆　　◆　　◆

A little more than a year after Barbara and I arrived, I stood in the front section of Broadway Carpet Service chatting with the Armstrong Linoleum salesman. He came in weekly. We would go over our inventory and figure out what patterns were running low and needed to be reordered, or he would show me some new patterns that were being introduced. Unexpectedly Larry said, "Do you mind if I ask you a personal question?"

"No. What's on your mind?"

He took a deep breath, "I know it's none of my business, but I have to ask why you stay here. Why don't you move into a nicer neighborhood and open a store there? This neighborhood's not going to get any better."

I had come to know Larry fairly well. He was well aware of my employment history starting with the *Monitor*. I could see where he was coming from. But I replied, "There's not much likelihood of that. My father and uncle have been here since 1934. They're not going to change."

Around 6:00 PM that same day, Barbara came into the store. She had left her office in Times Square at 5:00 PM, taken the IRT to 157th Street, gotten off, and walked from Broadway up 157th to Amsterdam Avenue where she had turned left, and walked some two hundred feet to Broadway Carpet. She and I headed home. My father would lock up later. We walked back down 157th Street to the subway station.

Our crowded train came in quickly, and we stepped on. We hung onto the ceiling straps and swayed back and forth along with everyone else. I told Barbara about my conversation with Larry.

"Did his question surprise you?"

"Strangely, no. I mean it was odd that he would ask such a question of one of his customers, I suppose. But not the question itself."

"So you've been wondering the same thing?"

"Not about opening a store someplace else. Although it's an interesting idea. It's just that I have to admit I don't see much of a future for us here."

"God. I'm glad to hear you say that, Bob. You know I don't like where we live and I don't like where either of us works. I was thinking about it as I walked up to the store. I hate that walk. I'm the only white person on that street, to say nothing of being a woman. I feel all those eyes watching me as I walk by. It's very unsettling."

"Yeah. I know you feel that way. Somehow I don't worry about it."

"That's because you're not a woman, and you've basically lived here all your life. And then there's my own job. I hate the commute to Times Square. And most of the men at work are a bunch of pigs. All they do is chase the women around their desks. I hate it."

Soon our train came to 242nd Street. "So what are we going to do?" I said as we walked along the platform toward the exit and took a long flight of stairs down to our bus stop.

"Let me ask you," Barbara said as we waited for our bus to arrive, "Do you like our present situation?"

"I had no idea how things were going to work out after we arrived here. But I honestly thought our coming to New York was a demonstration. It sure seemed like an answer to our prayers. I came down here thinking that somehow there would be a future for us. Why else were we here if not to see some opportunity for growth? But it's not to be. The business is slowly dying."

"And so ...?" Barbara asked.

"And so, I don't know," I said.

As we got off the bus Barbara said, "Well, I think I do know. We could go back to New England. You know my father has said he'd love to have us join him."

"But what would I say to Mom and Dad?"

"Your mother knows perfectly well what the situation is. She and I do talk, you know. She'll understand. I don't know about your father."

As we approached the front steps of our home I stopped and faced Barbara. "He's not going to be happy."

"I don't suppose he is. On the other hand, he knows I don't like it here. Of course, he thinks my queasiness is funny. I'm just a country hick. But he knows."

◆   ◆   ◆

We visited my parents that following Sunday. I had telephoned earlier to let them know we were coming over. I felt very uneasy.

"Dad, I'm afraid I have to tell you that Barbara's father has offered us a job in Rockport, and we've accepted his offer."

The four of us had congregated in the living room. Dad was sitting in the wingback chair he and I had electrified all those years ago. He had lowered his paper to his lap when we entered the room. When I told him, he looked at me and Barbara, and I had the feeling he was not surprised. "Let me see if I understand you," he said. "I bailed you out of your fiasco in North Reading. You've gotten back on your feet. So now you're going to just leave. Do I have that right?"

"I can understand why you'd see it that way. And we're very grateful for your help. But we just don't see any future here."

"Well, I never believed my own son would pull a stunt like this. But I guess you have to do what you have to do." With that he picked up his paper and continued to read.

◆   ◆   ◆

About a year and a half from the time we left North Reading, we were back in New England living with my in-laws in Rockport. Within three months of our arrival in Rockport, I followed Larry's advice, and went into the floor covering business, representing three building trades stores on Cape Ann. I also helped out at the hotel from time to time while Barbara worked full time.

I was relieved once we got back to New England. It seemed to me that there was so much more light. Broadway Carpet had become dark. I had never seen it that way when working there in my earlier years. But now? I couldn't quite put my finger on what was happening. What was that darkness that seemed to be enveloping the place? I could not see myself following in my father's footsteps. He spent such long hours there while the rest of us went home. Somehow, I knew he would stay at 1968 Amsterdam Avenue until the day he died.

But I did carry a sense of guilt. My mother and my wife told me not to. "Feeling guilty never does anyone any good." they said. Still, when you've disappointed your father you do carry that guilt, no matter how reasonable your actions may have felt.

OCTOBER 19, 1972

Barbara let me go first. I stepped into the office but was stopped by my father's body. His head was no more than two feet from where I was standing. He was lying on his stomach. His arms were at his sides. His legs extended straight back into the office. His face was on its side. There was a large gash on the top of his head. Blood had radiated out from his head into the green, flat indoor/outdoor carpet.

Barbara gasped, "Oh my God!"

I went numb. I could not look anymore. I turned around, and headed back into the store. Barbara took my hand. "Are you all right?" she asked. I could only slightly nod.

Suddenly, the front door opened. Three detectives came in. One was Detective Rochford, an older man with a gentle demeanor. The other two were much younger—jocks, really. My father's body lay about twenty-five feet to my left. The detectives quizzed us regarding how we arrived here. I explained that we traveled all night from Rockport.

"Why," I wondered to myself, "are they asking me these questions? Are they looking for an alibi? Can they think I might have done this?"

Then I asked: "How did this happen?"

"Your father was hit on the head with a carpet kicker," Rochford answered. "You know what that is?"

"Jesus! Yeah, I know what that is," I answered. A carpet kicker is a very heavy eighteen inch long tool that carpet installers use. One end has an approximately five inch square heavy metal head on it with thick sharply pointed needles that extend out of the bottom of the head. The installer presses the needles into the carpet. The other end is cushioned and is struck by the installer with his knee to move the carpet into position.

"Do you have any idea who did this?" I asked.

"Only one. David Johnston. You know him?"

"David? Yes I know him. I used to work with him. He was a good guy."

"Maybe then," one of the jocks said. "Your father's secretary told us your father just fired him because he was on drugs. We rousted him out of bed last night. Made him strip down. Looked under his fingernails. Even looked up his asshole. Couldn't find anything, but if he did it, we'll get him."

"Jesus. So you've spoken to Eleanor? Do you know when my father was killed?"

"We won't know for certain until the medical examiner gets here," Rochford answered. "All we know is that Mrs. Harris says she left the store last night at six like she always does, and your father locked the door behind her. He said he'd be heading home shortly after her. So it was some time after six."

"But my mother didn't find him until two o'clock this morning. I don't get it."

"It was 1:45 AM. We got the call at two."

"You mean my Dad's been lying there all this time, and the medical examiner hasn't gotten here yet?"

"Afraid so. It's been a busy night."

"Christ." I paused a second, then asked, "Do you really think you're going to find whoever did this?"

"Oh, we'll get the guy," one of the younger detectives said. "You can bet the neighborhood knows who did it. They always do. We'll get the guy. We'll roust every bar. We'll find out."

"Well, thanks for coming down Mr. Ellis," Rochford said. "We'll let you know when we learn something." They turned toward the door, nodded to the patrolman who had been standing nearby, and left. Barbara and I followed them out, leaving my father's body in the care of the lone policeman.

◆   ◆   ◆

Forty minutes later, we were back in Yonkers.

"How are you doing, Mother?" I asked as we entered her living room. She was resting on her couch with her head propped up on the arm and her *Science and Health* in her lap.

"I'm better now that you're here. Did you see Daddy?"

"Yes. Mother, there's something Barbara and I can't understand. How was it that you had to find Dad's body? Why were you in that neighborhood at 2:00 AM?"

"Well, it's pretty disgraceful the way the police handled things."

"What do you mean?"

"I arrived home at about seven o'clock. Usually, Daddy arrives about the same time. He wasn't here, so I decided to lie down until he got home. I must have been very tired, though, because it was nine o'clock when I woke up. There was no sign of your father so I called the factory, but there was no answer. I didn't know what to do. So, I waited until 10:00 PM before I finally decided to call the Thirty-second Precinct.

"I asked the desk sergeant to have someone check the factory. He said he would and that he'd call me back, but he didn't. At eleven o'clock, I called again. The sergeant said they hadn't gotten to it. I pleaded with him to go check. He said he would have someone look. By midnight I still had heard nothing, so I called again. I was feeling very nervous now, and yet the sergeant had the gall to tell me that I shouldn't worry. He said that Daddy probably was out on a toot in one of the bars. 'Now listen to me, young man,' I said. 'This is a seventy-two-year-old white man. He is not out on a toot, not in that neighborhood, not anywhere. He should have been home long before now. You go check on his store. It's only a block from where you are!'

"'All right,' the man said, but he never called back.

"Then, at one o'clock, I heard our tenant Phil come in downstairs. He works nights, you know. I asked him to drive me down to the factory. When we got there we found the gate to the store wide open, the lights on, and the front door flapping in the breeze. I ran into the store and found Daddy lying on the floor in the office. I yelled, 'Phil, get the police. James has been mugged!' Phil drove the block or so to the Thirty-second Precinct. I kneeled next to Daddy, and stroked his back saying 'It's all right now, James. Help is coming.' I kept saying it over and over. Phil found a patrol car parked in front of the police station with two patrolmen in it drinking coffee. He yelled at them to follow him and made a U-turn.

"I still was kneeling beside Daddy when I felt someone grab my shoulders and pull me up. 'It's okay, Mrs. Ellis,' I heard. 'We'll take care of him now.' They led me into the store area and sat me down on a chair. Phil told me to call you. I was looking down at the floor as I spoke to you and said that Daddy had been mugged. Then I saw two polished shoes in front of me. I looked up and saw that it was one of the patrolmen. He was shaking his head.

"That's when you said, 'Oh, Bobby, he's dead. Daddy's dead,'"

"Yes."

"That's disgusting," Barbara said. "I can't believe they put you through that."

"I can't either," my mom said. "Although I have to say that once the police got there they were very nice and helpful."

◆   ◆   ◆

On Monday afternoon, October 23, 1972, I stood in the middle of the main floor of the factory surrounded by thirty-eight years of floor covering paraphernalia. It had been five days since my mother found my father's body, five days since I first saw his body.

I began to wonder, "Were you standing here Dad? Before they knocked?"

Suddenly I heard my cousin Lee exclaim, "Oh my!"

He had just seen the blood soaked into the dark green indoor/outdoor carpet on the office floor.

"Jesus," I heard from my cousin John

I could not go in there. I felt as though I was in a bubble. I heard. I saw. But I had become an automaton.

Lee had flown up from Nashville, Tennessee. He, John, my mother, Barbara, and I met at Aunt Dorothy's home in Leonia, New Jersey. Then my two cousins and I drove across the George Washington Bridge and to the factory. Their father, my Uncle Leroy and Dad's partner, had died two years earlier of natural causes.

Now, as I stood on this main floor I wondered, "Or were you in the office, Dad? That's where they killed you. But you were supposed to be closing up. You must have come out here. You had to turn off these lights. Didn't you? They weren't on when Mom found you. You must have stood where I am now, reached for the light cord, and pulled it. Such a simple act. You've done it thousands of times. Then you entered the office through its back entrance."

I turned in place, and stared at the room. It was bright daylight outside but in here it was gray. A few rays filtered in through the three dirty, barred, tall windows that looked out on the courtyard. Through the filth I could make out the backs of brick apartment buildings.

"Did anybody see you in here, Dad? Neighbors once called the police when they saw burglars trying to get in. Not this time. If they saw anything, they're not telling."

I saw all the empty shelving, which used to hold thousands of rugs. They went from the floor to the twenty-foot high ceiling. I saw the sewing machine in the repair area where Mrs. Lundquist used to sew rugs. I saw the huge old wine casks, which held soap for the cleaning of rugs downstairs. I saw the back door to the office. I smelled the must, the dust of age. The place was so dark, so lonely, so sad.

I continued silently questioning my father, "So you went into the office. Then you heard a knock on the front door to the store. It must have been very loud. It's fifty feet from where you were. Or were you in the store? All the lights up front were on. But why? What could have kept you here? You were supposed to be going home."

I wandered past the office to the front of the narrow fifty-foot-long store. I turned around and looked back at the office and the bank-teller-type window where people paid their bills. I saw Lee and John leaving the office. They had the blood-soaked carpet in their hands. They were carrying it at arms-length out to the back where the trash is kept.

"How did it happen, Dad? How could anyone have gotten in and done this to you?"

My cousins returned. "Well, we'd better have a look around," Lee said.

"Where should we start?" John wondered aloud as he started turning around. We were in the middle of the floor out back—the floor of what used to be a movie theater back in the 1920s and the floor of the building where my father spent almost every day of my life.

"Maybe we should start downstairs," Lee suggested.

We headed over to a hole in the floor; it was a trapdoor with stairs reaching down to the basement below. Lee pulled a string, several lights went on and John and I followed Lee down. There were no windows down here. Only more shelving, a few scattered rugs, the carpet beater, the old wash floor, scrubbing machines, ringer, dry-room with its gas-fired heater, which I always thought looked like a jet engine. We walked around the entire area stepping over the occasional rug. Lee asked, "How come there still are rugs here?"

"I suppose they never got claimed," John responded.

The carpet cleaning end of the business had been sold several years earlier.

"Nothing much of value down here," Lee concluded.

We headed back upstairs. It was such familiar territory for all of us. We were raised here. Our fathers worked in this building servicing the neighborhood since 1934, the year John and I were born. After Uncle Leroy died, Dad and my Aunt Dorothy continued the business. Until now.

"So this is it, Daddy. This is the end." I thought.

We walked around the perimeter of the main floor where Dad and Aunt Dorothy had turned some space into sort of a sales area. A display of carpet samples stood below the dirty windows. A large rack that held nine-by-twelve-foot rugs was suspended from the wall. Several rugs were spread out in the center, destined to be worked on for some customer.

We went through the back door to the office. The tile floor now was bare. The cash register still was covered with fingerprint dust. Papers were scattered about the desk surfaces. There was a brown stain where my father's head had lain and his blood had bled through the carpet. It was all I could do to stand there.

We walked out the front door of the office toward the front store area. Here we found at least one hundred rolls of linoleum of all sizes, patterns, and colors. The rolls stood on end. Some were six feet tall, some nine feet, some twelve feet. The twelve-footers came close to reaching the ceiling. They were in rows extending out from one wall, like stacks in a library.

"Man. There's a lot of stuff here!" John exclaimed.

"Indeed there is," Lee replied.

"I guess we need to take an inventory," John said.

"Now?" I asked, sounding startled.

"No. But how about later?" John looked at me.

"Yeah, sure. But I'm a little confused right now. We have to go to the morgue tomorrow. Then there are arrangements for my father. Let me give you a call."

"The morgue?" John's eyes widened.

"Yes, to identify the body."

"Jesus. It's hard to believe, isn't it?" John said as he stared at me and then moved his gaze over to Lee. "I mean, to think it all would have come to this."

"I haven't even begun to understand what has happened," I replied.

"Nor I," John added.

We turned off the lights, exited the front door, locked its three deadbolts, pulled the gate across the front, and locked it with two heavy-duty padlocks. We walked to my car around the corner on 157th Street, climbed in, and drove back to Leonia.

◆   ◆   ◆

Sunday, Oct. 29, 1972, 11:00 AM. It had been ten days since Dad was killed. Barbara, my mother, and I entered the small chapel, which was part of a massive mausoleum at Ferncliff Cemetery in Hartsdale, about twenty miles from Yonkers. There was seating for seventy-five to one hundred, but we were the only mourners. Dad was not a Christian Scientist, so holding some sort of CS service wouldn't have seemed appropriate. And he always said he wanted no muss, no fuss when he died. Besides, Mrs. Eddy made no provision for funerals in her church. Now, at the front of this gothic chapel, his coffin sat on a draped platform. We sat perhaps ten rows back. I was on the aisle. Mother was next to me. Barbara was next to her.

I had returned to my bubble. It was all so unreal; beyond anything I had ever experienced. I had been moving through molasses from one event to the next and thinking how these events were all set in motion with the strike of a carpet kicker on my father's head.

We had just come from the Phillips Funeral Home on South Broadway in Yonkers where three days ago we sat in front of the funeral director making arrangements. "I'm afraid I have to ask you a question," he said to my mother. "I have the tag that was used to identify your husband's body at the morgue. Would you like to have it?"

"No," my mother replied.

"Well, it's just that we want you to be certain that we have the correct body. The New York morgue at Bellevue has been known to make mistakes."

"Oh," Mother replied. She was silent for a moment. Then she continued, "Well, you're certain aren't you?"

"Oh, yes," the director said. "The tag definitely has your husband's name on it—James R. Ellis."

"Then let's leave it at that," Mom said.

It was silent in the chapel, except for a dull roar that seemed to be coming from behind the front platform. "What is that sound?" I wondered to myself. We sat silently. We had made no formal plans for a service.

"What can we say, Daddy? Where will we ever find any answers?" I silently asked.

"Our Father which art in heaven," Mother began to intone. "Hallowed be thy name," Barbara and I joined in. "Thy Kingdom come. Thy will be done on earth as it is in heaven. Give us this day our daily bread, and forgive us our debts, as we forgive our debtors. And lead us not into temptation, but deliver us from evil; for thine is the kingdom, and the power, and the glory, forever."

My head was bowed, with my chin almost touching my chest. Barbara sat in a similar position. However, Mother sat erect. Her hands were clasped in her lap, her face was pointed straight ahead, and her eyes were closed.

"Life is eternal," Mother recited from *Science and Health*. "We should find this out and begin the demonstration thereof. Life and goodness are immortal. Let us then shape our views of existence into loveliness, freshness, and continuity, rather than into age and blight … Man is not the offspring of flesh, but of Spirit—of Life, not of matter. Because Life is God, Life must be eternal, self-existent. Life is the everlasting I AM, the Being who was and is and shall be, whom nothing can erase."[1]

I said nothing. Barbara remained silent.

"The Lord is my shepherd; I shall not want," Mother continued. We joined her. "He maketh me to lie down in green pastures; he leadeth me beside the still waters. He restoreth my soul; he leadeth me in the paths of righteousness for his name's sake. Yea, though I walk through the valley of the shadow of death, I will fear no evil for thou art with me; thy rod and thy staff they comfort me. Thou preparest a table before me in the presence of mine enemies; thou anointest my head with oil; my cup runneth over. Surely goodness and mercy shall follow me all the days of my life, and I will dwell in the house of the Lord forever."

"God almighty, Dad! Where is the solace I am supposed to be feeling? Why do these words do nothing for me? Why is your body up there in that Goddamn box?"

There was utter silence except for that dull roar coming from behind the altar. Suddenly, as if on cue though none of us had moved, Dad's coffin started moving. Slowly it proceeded toward the rear, through a curtain, which the coffin displaced. The curtain fell back in place. The coffin was gone.

"Has that roar become louder?" I wondered. "Good-bye, Daddy."

---

1.   *S&H*: Pages 246 and 289

IN MEMORIAM

Two weeks later, on Sunday, November 12, 1972, I stood with my back to a roll of linoleum. There were one hundred people or so in the store. John was out back. He and I were having a sale. We had hired an off-duty plainclothes detective to stand guard at the door. His name was Gonzales, a cheerful man with two revolvers—one short nose for short range, one long for long range. Just before we opened the doors, he showed them to us and explained how they worked. He liked his job.

Now customers were going back and forth. They pointed at a linoleum remnant, and asked, "How much?"

"Five dollars," I said. Or I quoted another price, depending on the size of the remnant.

"Okay" they said.

I handed it to them, and they handed me the money.

The detectives working on my father's case had learned I was back in town. They, Gonzales, and I were standing near the front door. "Well, we know how your father died," Rochford said. "I mean besides the fact that he was hit on the head. We know, for instance, that he never felt anything."

"How do you know that?" I asked.

"It's the way he fell. Did you notice how his arms were at his sides? If he had been conscious when he fell, he would have tried to break his fall. His hands and arms would have been above his head. We also now know there were two men involved, and your father had to know at least one of them because he wouldn't have let anyone in unless he did. And he *had* locked up behind Mrs. Harris. She's sure of that. So he hears the knock on the door shortly after she leaves. I don't know if we told you but the medical examiner set the time of death at 6:30."

"Christ, that means he was here, in this store, with the place wide open from 6:30 PM until my mother found him at 1:45 AM, and nobody saw anything?"

"I know. It doesn't make any sense. In any case, your father goes up front, sees this guy he knows, and lets him in. He also lets in the second guy who your father may or may not know. Must be about 6:15. They follow him back toward the office. He goes into the front door to the office and then to the pay window. He's leaning with his elbows on the window ledge talking to the guy he knows who is facing him on the other side of the window. Meantime, the second guy backs up into the shadows. He sneaks around to the back door to the office. He sees the carpet kicker in with the other tools that are right there, picks it up, and goes through the back door to the office, which was not locked.

"Now your father was partially deaf, so he doesn't hear the guy sneaking up on him. And he had no peripheral vision, so he can't see the guy out of the corner of his eyes. The guy strikes him very hard on the head with the kicker. The pair rifle through the cash register and get a few pennies. Mrs. Harris says everything was in the safe all locked up. They take his watch and wallet and leave."

"Your wrist watch, Dad? Armstrong Floors gave it to you because you sold a bunch of linoleum. What was it worth, do you suppose? Maybe twenty-five dollars?" I wondered silently.

"What do you mean, he had no peripheral vision?" I asked.

"Didn't they tell you?"

"Didn't who tell me?"

"The morgue. He had a large brain tumor. He was going blind."

The morgue. Mother, Barbara, and I had gone to Belleview to view the body. "Would you do it, Bobby?" Mother had asked. She and Barbara stayed in the waiting room. I was led downstairs to a picture window with a curtain pulled across it. The curtains parted.

"That explains it," I said.

"Explains what?" Rochford asked.

"When I looked at his face at the morgue it was positively grotesque. They must have put it back together after cutting his head open, but nobody said anything to me. The pathologist only asked me if my father was having problems with his eyes. All I knew was that he wore glasses. The pathologist only nodded and left. I asked my mother about it. She said he had been having trouble with his eyes; he'd been to an optometrist and had gotten new glasses, but they weren't helping. He was disgusted. But a tumor? Going blind? I'm certain she had no idea whatsoever. She would have told me. I wonder if my father knew and just didn't want to tell her. Wouldn't an optometrist think something was really wrong if he found you had no peripheral vision? Wouldn't he say something to you?"

"You'd think so," Rochford answered.

Out of the corner of my eye, I saw a guy leaving the store with a rug I knew he had not paid for. "Did you buy that?" I asked him.

"Yeah," he said.

I yelled to John who was out back, "Did you sell that Karastan?"

"No," he yelled back.

The guy pulled out a knife. There were three representatives of the New York City Police Department talking to me, and Gonzales was at the front door. Gonzales opened his jacket revealing his two pistols.

"You don't wanna die over something like that," Gonzales said.

The guy dropped the rug and ran.

"Well, we'd better let you carry on here, but give us a ring if anything comes up." Rochford said.

◆   ◆   ◆

By three o'clock that afternoon the store had emptied out.

Gonzales said, "Why don't you guys gather together the money, and I'll walk you to your car, just to be sure." Great idea. We put the money in a brown paper bag, exited the store, locked up, and walked to our car.

I dropped John off at his apartment on W. Eighty-first Street, and I headed back to Yonkers. When I got there my mother was saying over the phone, "Thank you, John. I'll tell him." She hung up, turned to me, and said, "You took in three thousand dollars."

"Oh, good." I replied.

"I took another phone call before John's," she continued. "The neighborhood wants to hold a memorial service for Daddy. They want to know if we would attend. I told them I'd talk to you. It's being organized by the minister at the Methodist church next door to the police station. He called me. He sounds very nice. He said the neighborhood is all upset over what happened, including what happened to me."

"How do they know about that?" I asked.

"I honestly don't know, but they do."

"What do you think?"

"I think we should go. All those good people. He was the last white merchant in the neighborhood, you know. That's what Rev. Williams said. 'And he didn't desert us,' is what he told me. 'He did so much for us. He was always willing to donate whatever he could for a drug clinic or a homeless shelter. You'd see him in some storefront on his own hands and knees installing a piece of linoleum.' He sounded very moved. They want to give him a proper memorial."

◆   ◆   ◆

Saturday night, Nov. 18, it was exactly one month since Dad's murder. Aunt Dorothy, John, Mother, Barbara, and I sat in the front pew of this packed Methodist church on the corner of 155th Street and Amsterdam Ave.—next door to the Thirty-second Precinct.

Bella Abzug was speaking from the pulpit. She followed Rev. Williams who spoke eloquently about my father. Now Bella—a member of the House of Representatives, representing the people of Harlem—was ranting at the New York City Police Department and specifically the members of the Thirty-second Precinct.

"What the hell is this woman doing here at this service?" I asked myself. "She didn't know Dad."

Then I heard her words. She was reciting my mother's ordeal. "Where were the police?" Bella asked. Over and over as she went through the events she repeated the question, "Where were the police?"

"Where were they at 6:30?" Bella wanted to know. "Where were they at 9:00?" She continued to go through the clock up to 2:00 AM where she had it that the police finally responded to my mother's pleas.

"How," she asked, "can this neighborhood have any confidence in their police department when not even this elderly white man got any attention. We can't even know if he might have lived had the police done their jobs. He lay there in that store, the front door wide open, the lights on, blood pouring out of his head, from 6:30 on while New York's finest were having coffee in their squad car not one block away. Where were the police?"

"Jesus, Dad. Did you live after they struck you? My God! I never thought of that." I asked myself.

I looked at Mother. She was looking toward Bella, but I had a feeling her eyes were on some distant object.

Finally, Rev. Williams gave a benediction, and we all stood up. I turned around, and saw hundreds of black faces looking at us. I began to recognize some of them. Many were smiling shyly. They began to come forward. One by one they shook my hand.

"Hi, Mr. Richardson. Thanks so much for coming," I said. I had called on this man several times over the years. He was such a nice, older man. We embraced.

"Hello, Mrs. Smith," I said as I received a peck on the cheek, and I felt tears welling up in my eyes.

"Hello, Mrs. Brown," I said as I received another peck. I had forgotten all these good people—Dad's customers.

"Are you here Dad? Do you see all these people?" I asked silently.

Then I heard the words, "Mr. Ellis, can we talk with you for a minute?" I turned to see bright lights shining on me, and I was staring into a television camera. "I'm from Channel 5. I wonder if I could ask you a few questions," the reporter said as he pried me away from the congregants.

"Are you bitter?" he asked.

"Am I bitter?" I wondered to myself.

Then I answered, "No, I'm not bitter. If I allow my thought to drop to that level and become bitter, then I become sick too. That's not what's needed here. That kind of thinking never helped anyone. Look around at these people. They don't need bitterness. They don't need vengeance. They … *we* need healing. We need to get at the root of what allowed these events to take place, and fix it."

The reporter quickly turned to my mother.

"Are *you* bitter?" he asked.

"No, I'm not bitter," Mother responded without hesitation. "I have a religion that won't let me be bitter."

"You have a religion?"

"Yes. And it only allows me to look forward with hope. I have to know that somehow healing will come of this. I know we have heard a lot of ugly words tonight. But we also have heard of the need for love and caring. We've experienced it at this service. Haven't you?" she asked as she looked at the reporter. "Ultimately," she continued, "there has to be a way of looking at this situation that will allow a sense of healing to take place, and where all elements in the neighborhood, including the police, can pull together through a sense of what I call universal Love. I'm speaking of the love of God, which must be allowed to embrace all of us right here in this church and this neighborhood right now, regardless of who we are or what we have done. That is how we may begin to see real change take place."

"Thank you," the reporter said. Then he turned to his camera.

We began to leave when another man approached.

"Mrs. Ellis? My name is Jim Donahue. I'm from the Public Information Office of the Police Department. I've heard tonight for the first time some pretty serious allegations about how you were treated the night your husband was killed. I've spoken with Internal Affairs, and they wondered if you would be willing to answer some questions."

"Well, yes. I suppose that would be all right," Mother responded.

"Would it be possible for us to talk with you tonight?"

"Tonight? My goodness. It's ten o'clock. I'd really like to get home."

"That's fine. We'd be happy to come to your home. It shouldn't take more than a half hour. We just want to get the facts straight from you."

"Why not, Mother?" I asked. "They do need to have the information. And, if they'll come out to Yonkers, that'll save you having to come back down here."

"Well, I suppose you're right." she said as she turned to the policeman. "All right. You come on out. We should be back there in about an hour."

◆   ◆   ◆

One week later I was back in Yonkers. Mother and I were getting ready to pack up the last items we wanted from Broadway Carpet. Mother handed me a letter and said, "Look at this."

The letter read:

Dear Mrs. Ellis,

I have asked the people at Channel Five to forward this letter to you.

I am a Roman Catholic. I don't know what your religion is. It doesn't matter.

I heard you interviewed after your husband's memorial service. I can only say I have never before heard such a courageous and healing statement on the TV. We can only hope that our elected officials heard it too. Would that we all could behave as you have.

Thank you so much.

I looked at Mother. "I've received several of these," she said. "They were sent to the television station and they forwarded them to me. It's really quite wonderful, isn't it?"

"Yes. It is."

We had watched the eleven o'clock news after arriving back in Yonkers after the memorial service and had seen Bella Abzug quoted and then Mother's complete interview.

Soon after the news, three men from Internal Affairs plus Jim Donahue arrived. We sat in Mother's living room. Mother answered their questions giving them the times she had called the Thirty-second Precinct and the steps she finally had taken. After they had gathered the information they needed they asked: "Mrs. Ellis do you want to press charges?"

"That thought hadn't occurred to me," she said. After reflecting for a moment she added, "No. I don't see any purpose in that. Just you make certain that something like this cannot happen again. Make certain that when someone calls the Thirty-second Precinct, or any precinct in New York, and the desk sergeant answers the phone, make certain that he and the rest of the men there will act appropriately and promptly. Can you do that?"

"We can sure try, Mrs. Ellis. It may take a while. But we can sure try." One of the men responded.

"Well. I suggest you do more than try. You're intelligent people," she said sounding as though she were lecturing one of her patients. "You wouldn't be where you are now if that weren't the case. You can make it happen. Or your superiors can. You tell them. You make certain they understand that there are a whole lot of people looking for change, and it's not just the people in that neighborhood. You do understand. Don't you?"

"Yes, ma'am. We sure do. And thank you again for your time." They rose from their seats, left Mother's living room, walked quietly downstairs, and exited out the front door. We never heard from them again.

In fact, we never heard from the police again. Not the detectives. Not anyone. Not a word. Dad's murder was one of five homicides in New York City that night. Such a busy night.

We went back to Rockport. My mother too. Every now and then Mom sits with her books in her lap, and wonders to me, "What do you suppose Daddy's thinking right now?"

I sometimes ask myself as well. "Are you thinking, Dad? Are you aware that I did finally come out of the bubble? I have cried. I'm so sorry I disappointed you. I know I did—in so many ways, especially when we left and headed back to Rockport. But I couldn't help it, Dad. Barbara and I couldn't stay in Harlem. There was no future there. Not for any of us. You do see that now. Don't you?"

The factory is gone now; it was torn down by the city of New York. All those empty shelves, the scrubbing machines, the beater, the ringer, the dry room, the dirty windows, the empty rug racks, the must, and the dust, it's all gone—replaced by the Thurgood Marshall Plaza apartment building built by the City of New York for the very residents Broadway Carpet had served. Marshall was the first African American Supreme Court justice. My father would have approved.

PART II

ADOPTION

"Why don't we call the New England Home?" I asked Barbara.

"Why bother? It's been five years," she responded. "We know why they haven't called us."

"We don't really know. We only think we know."

"Oh, we know all right," Barbara said referring to the fact that my former co-writer at the *Monitor,* Dana Gatlin, now a freelance writer, had written an article for the *Boston Globe* in which he examined the trials and tribulations of childless couples who sought adoptions. He interviewed us as well as others. He quizzed several adoption agencies, including the New England Home for Little Wanderers in Jamaica Plain, a suburb of Boston where we had applied to adopt a child. One question he raised was, "What is your policy regarding placing babies into various religious settings?" The answers made it seem clear that Christian Science couples stood little chance of receiving a baby.

We had applied to the New England Home five years ago and gone through a series of interviews. Suddenly everything had inexplicably stopped. Then we moved to New York.

Soon after arriving in New York, we decided to apply to the Spence Chapin Adoption Agency in Manhattan. They insisted that we have tests to determine whether or not there was a physical impediment to our having a child. This meant going to doctors and having tests done—not a normal procedure for a Christian Scientist.

We had been praying over our situation for all these years with no results. Still, we believed we had been led by Divine Mind to go the adoption route. We had had no success at the New England Home. We didn't know why that was. But now we were here at Spence Chapin. We had always understood that sometimes it is necessary to take certain human footsteps to accomplish God's plan for us. We had come this far. It wouldn't be legitimate to stop at this point, we felt.

There were impediments, it turned out, and a highly experimental artificial insemination procedure was suggested. Procedures that are almost commonplace today had not been discovered in 1969. This meant that both Barbara and I would have to go into the hospital. Once again, we decided to follow those human footsteps that appeared to have been pointed out to us. The procedure did not work. Now we were in Rockport and somewhat at a loss. March 4, 1970, would mark our ninth wedding anniversary.

"You know," I now said to Barbara, "it's been like walking on eggshells with the adoption agencies because we're so concerned over possibly doing something to give cause to reject our application. Dana's article indicated that all prospective adoptive parents have that fear. But it's been five years. I'm going to call The New England Home For Little Wanderers."

After taking down our information, the receptionist told me that our social worker had retired. A new woman would return our call.

A Ms. Engleton telephoned us the next day. "We owe you a huge apology," she said. "There was another couple by the name of Mr. and Mrs. Ellis who applied around the same time as you applied, and they later withdrew their application. Yours was pulled as well by mistake. I hate to have to ask you this. I know you went through this process once already. But could you come in and reapply?"

Two days later Barbara and I returned to Jamaica Plain.

After about six weeks of interviews, which ended with a visit from Ms. Engleton to our little apartment at the Yankee Clipper Inn in Rockport, she said, "I can't say exactly when. But you'll be hearing from us. I promise we won't lose your application this time."

We heard nothing more from Ms. Engleton until the first week in June 1970. "Can you come into our offices?" she asked.

On Wednesday, June 10, 1970, we entered, yet again, the offices of the New England Home for Little Wanderers. Ms. Engleton brought us into a small room. "I'll be right back," she said.

We stood silently in the little room looking at each other not quite certain what was going to happen. Suddenly, Ms. Engleton returned. In her arms was a tiny baby wrapped in a blue blanket. Golden blond hair peeked out from under a blue cap. His eyes were closed. He was sound asleep. Ms. Engleton had a huge smile on her face. "Would you like to hold him?" she asked as she handed the baby to Barbara. "I'll leave you three alone for a bit," Ms. Engleton said as she left the room, quietly closing the door behind her.

Barbara held this tiny child in her arms. Tears rolled down her cheeks. She looked up at me. "Do you want to hold him?" she asked as she handed him to me. Tears formed in my eyes.

Somewhere during the interview process we had gotten it into our heads that if this happened we would be given three days to decide if we wanted the child. I said to Barbara, "There's no way I can leave here without this baby."

"Me too."

At that moment, Ms. Engleton came back in the room, and I blurted out, "Can we take him home?"

"Of course you can. Why do you think you're here?" she asked.

We were speechless.

Ms. Engleton said that this little boy was ten days old. "There was a staph infection at the hospital he was born in," she explained. "We had to wait until that was cleared up before we could bring him here. Otherwise I would have called you sooner." She took the baby from Barbara and placed him in a bassinet. Then she put a bottle full of formula next to him, handed me a package of diapers and some baby clothes, walked us out to our car, put the baby in Barbara's lap after she was seated, and wished us well.

I climbed into the driver's seat and stared at our new baby boy in my wife's lap. "I can't believe this," I said. "After all these years, it's unbelievable."

"He's so beautiful," was all Barbara could say as I started the car and we drove off.

◆　　　◆　　　◆

We named our little boy Jeffrey Scott Ellis. For years we wondered over what events could have brought about his arrival in our home after so many frustrating years of working with two adoption agencies. We wondered if Dana's article had put the New England Home in an embarrassing position. Had they really lost our application? Perhaps Ms. Engleton, who was much younger than the first social worker, made the difference.

Whatever the reason, we believed that God had brought this child to us, and we were extremely grateful. Thirty-four years later, Jeffrey started a search for his birth mother. He located her, and now is in touch with her. We, too, have spent some time with her and we now have a new friend. She was very young when she gave birth to Jeff, and she was a Christian Scientist. She had requested that her baby be placed in a Christian Science home.

A TESTIMONY

At about 7:30 PM on the second Wednesday in June 1976, I walked up the steps and into our church. I was happily greeted by the lone usher, and I took my seat in the center of one of the pews toward the rear of the church. A couple of other earlier comers were already seated and smiled a greeting to me.

I cast my eyes about the sanctuary at the off-white colored walls with the small windows and at the curved ceiling with its graceful bronze chandelier. At the front was the small platform on which sat the podium from which the First Reader would preside. To my left on the wall behind the podium were the words, "Divine Love Always Has Met and Always Will Meet Every Human Need." On the right were the words, "Ye Shall Know the Truth and the Truth Shall Make You Free."

More people came in. The organist started playing a prelude. Soon, the First Reader came out. She sat behind the podium. At precisely 7:45 PM, the organist finished, and the First Reader rose. "Good evening," she said. "Let's sing Hymn No. 238." She read the first verse, then sat down. The organist played the hymn through once, and we all rose, sang, and sat back down.

The Reader announced that she would read citations from the Bible and then from *Science and Health*. These would be readings that she had chosen for this meeting.

After about fifteen minutes, the First Reader finished her citations. We all recited the Lord's Prayer, and sang a second hymn. Then she invited the members of the congregation to give any testimonies or remarks they wished to share about Christian Science. She closed her books and looked out at the congregation, waiting for someone to stand and say something.

Several people got up in succession and expressed their gratitude for various healings or new understandings.

Toward the end of the evening, I stood up. The First Reader smiled a greeting to me. I thanked her for her readings. Then I gave the following testimony:

"I attended a lecture at my twentieth college reunion last weekend that left me rather puzzled, I suppose. But, at the same time, it left me feeling very grateful. This lecture seemed to in some way verify my outlook on life, which I believe I have learned from Christian Science. However, this lecture had nothing to do with Christian Science or with any religion. It was given by the head of the physics department.

"The lecturer took us on a trip into a universe where, he said, our notions about that which is real, including our beliefs about time and about space, come into question.

"He began our journey by asking us to imagine an area in space where not even the greatest telescope can observe anything. None of the phenomena astronomers normally expect to detect when observing the heavens is in evidence. He called this void a black hole.

"Next, he told us that the concept of empty space is no longer valid. Albert Einstein and his theories of relativity have caused scientists to understand that space itself has properties. These properties are described by him in what is called the geometry of space-time. And so, according to the lecturer, the idea of a void in space is impossible.

"He told us that black holes are objects in space that are so dense and, therefore, have so much gravity that even particles as small as those that make up all forms of radiation, such as light, are forced into them. No particles can escape, and we, therefore, cannot see them. And, he said, it is speculated that black holes may be entrances into other universes. There may be an infinite number of universes, he said. I have to tell you I was blown away by that one.

"He asked us why we should care about black holes. Of what earthly importance could they be to us? He said they are important because such discoveries are founded on concepts that are completely foreign to those we were taught. These discoveries seem to defy everything we think we know about our three-dimensional world.

"Then he took us on a tour, as he called it, of the history of the physical sciences and of mankind's belief systems. He reminded us that during the age of myth when the Gods ruled in ancient Greece and elsewhere, people's beliefs were fact to them. Their universe as they understood it worked for them. He took us through later "universes" where people understood a universe in which the earth was at the center, and in which one God created and ruled all things. Later, he took us through a "mechanistic" universe in which Isaac Newton described a system where things worked like a machine—a machine that had been designed by God.

"We lived in this mechanistic universe, he explained, until the turn of the twentieth century—that was some three hundred years. And it worked for us.

Now Einstein's relativity plus quantum theory have created a very different universe in which *how we perceive things* becomes important.

"He told us that in quantum theory what they call subatomic particles (meaning particles that make up the atom) behave in such erratic ways that there's no predicting their behavior with 100 percent accuracy. It is only when we actually *observe* them that we can know for certain where they are and what they were doing. But, paradoxically, our act of observing them changes their very state. So we can't know for certain what their behavior might have been had we not disturbed them.

"In short, the very act of observation has altered the state of the object being observed. And this is now being extrapolated into the concept that all matter is basically very ethereal and the result of observation.

"He concluded by saying that a willingness on the part of scientific inquiry to broaden our horizons has introduced us in this century to a new way of thinking about ourselves, about our surroundings, about our earth, and about our universe. One does have to wonder, he said, what our next universe may embrace."

"Before I came here tonight, I looked up in my Concordance to Science and Health the word 'infinity'," I said as I pulled a piece of paper from my pocket.

"I came upon the following, 'Human capacity is slow to discern and to grasp God's creation and the divine power and presence which go with it demonstrating its spiritual origin. Mortals can never know the infinite, until they throw off the old man and reach the spiritual image and likeness.' Mrs. Eddy concludes by stating 'What can fathom infinity!'[1] Strangely, she ends that last statement with an exclamation point, not a question mark. I'm not certain what that signifies, unless she's telling us it's a huge subject. But I have to wonder. Do you suppose mankind is beginning to 'throw off the old man?'"

I sat down. Mine was the last testimony. The Reader announced a hymn. We all rose and sang. Then we exited and went to our various homes.

---

1. *S&H* 519:11

CARLY

At 8:05 AM on Monday, January 19, 1976, three months and five days since we had brought our newly adopted daughter home, our telephone rang. I answered it and said, "Hello?"

"Hello, Bob. This is Margaret Whitesill." Margaret Whitesill was the social worker at the Florence Crittenden League through whom we had adopted Carly, who now was seventeen months old.

"Hi, Margaret. How are you?" I asked as Carly sat in her highchair at the kitchen table. Barbara was feeding her some baby food, spiraling the spoon toward Carly's mouth while making airplane sounds.

"Well, I'm fine. But I'm afraid we have a problem," Margaret responded. I heard a large intake of breath, "We've received a complaint to the effect that your wife is unhappy with Carly."

"What? There has to be some mistake. Who made the complaint?"

"I'm not at liberty to say. But she is a reliable source with qualifications. I should add that it is only Mrs. Ellis about whom this complaint has been lodged."

Her voice was cold, unfriendly. This was not the same Margaret Whitesill we had come to know. She had warmly welcomed us at our first interview and encouraged us as we went through the process of applying to adopt a little girl from Medellin, Columbia. There never had been any question that our application would be accepted. She saw us through all the bureaucratic nuances, which we never would have been able to negotiate on our own. She visited us in our home several times, and we met with her in her home. Through it all, Margaret Whitesill had become a friend. But the tone of her voice now appeared to say otherwise.

"What sort of qualifications? I mean, this has to be someone who knows us. Doesn't it?"

"Well, her husband is a pediatrician and, yes, she has had some opportunity to learn directly what she has told me. I wonder if you could come to my office tomorrow."

"Hold on," I said as I put my hand over the mouthpiece, and told Barbara what had been said.

"What?!" she exclaimed. "Who would say such a thing?"

"I don't know. She says she can't tell us. She's asking if we can go to Lowell tomorrow. What do I say?"

"You say whatever you want. But this is an outrage."

"All right," I said to Mrs. Whitesill, "We'll be there. What time?"

We settled on a time and hung up.

Barbara's hand had remained poised in front of Carly. Carly's mouth still was open. Her dark brown, almost black, eyes were going back and forth between the two of us. Suddenly, Barbara turned away from me and continued feeding Carly but without the airplane sounds.

"What are we going to do?" I asked Barbara. "I have to tell you, there was an undertone in her voice that suggested that we could lose Carly."

"Shush, Bob. Not in front of her," Barbara said.

"Yeah, Right. But you know what I'm saying."

"What I don't understand," Barbara said, "is why she would believe some stranger and not rely on her own findings and our relationship with her. We had all those interviews, and we have our experience with Jeff."

We had adopted Jeff three and a half years earlier.

◆   ◆   ◆

Barbara was coming up the stairs from the family room as I walked in late that evening. She was holding Carly's hand. Jeff trailed behind.

"Hi, Daddy," Jeff called out.

"Hi Squirt," I said as I ruffled his hair. "And how's my little girl," I said as I picked up Carly, gave her a squeeze, and carried her into the kitchen. She had not learned to speak English comfortably yet. She understood what we said for the most part, but she still had problems articulating some words. "Hurroe, Daddy," she said as I nuzzled her neck. She gave me a slobbery kiss on the cheek in return. I set her down in her highchair, then sat down at the table, and turned to Barbara. "How're you doing?"

"To be honest, I'm feeling very angry. I've been thinking a lot about Margaret Whitesill," she said as she began to serve our dinner. She was used to my late evenings. A tuna fish casserole was in the oven. "I have to tell you that I am having a hard time not seeing this as a personal attack." She placed a plateful of casserole in front of me. "And I am incensed," Barbara continued, "that Margaret Whitesill would take in such an accusation without so much as a tiny doubt on her part."

"Well hopefully, that's why she wants to meet with us—to dispel any doubts she may have."

"Perhaps you're right," Barbara said. "But I'm telling you, I will not hear of any suggestion that—"

She stopped in mid-sentence. Then declared, "No one is going to take my—"

She looked in Carly's direction. "You know what I'm saying."

She was suggesting that the state might remove Carly from our home. As with Jeff's adoption, Carly remained a ward of the state during her first year with us. We had welcomed this concept when we adopted Jeff because it had released us from any question, as Christian Scientists, about the medical care of our child. Most Christian Science parents would not have made use of a pediatrician. We had to. And our experience with Jeff's pediatrician had been so positive that it never entered our mind not to continue with him after that first year. We brought Carly to him as well. I said, "Honey, there's absolutely no way we're even going to consider such a possibility."

"Well, just so you know, I consider this a personal affront, and I'm not going to stand for it. We're talking about my daughter, for God's sake."

"We're not talking about *your* daughter," I said. "We're talking about *our* daughter. Besides, we have no idea what Margaret is going to say tomorrow."

◆   ◆   ◆

I knew we needed some guidance, so I visited my mother. She had closed her office in Manhattan, sold her home in Yonkers, and moved last year into an apartment in Rockport just down the street from us. Many of her patients were in the New York City area and had visited her in her office, but most used the telephone. And she had many patients who were from as far away as California, Canada, and Europe. So she brought her telephone practice with her. Very quickly, local people started calling on her as well.

At this instant, I, in a way, was a patient calling on her. "Isn't it the darnedest thing," she said, "the way animal magnetism[1] will raise its ugly head just when we

---

1.   Reminder: In *S&H* 103:18 you read "As named in Christian Science, animal magnetism or hypnotism is the specific term for error, or mortal mind. It is the false belief that mind is in matter…" There is no matter in Christian Science. Any mortal mind suggestion to the contrary is *animal magnetism.*

feel things are going so well. You and Barbara have a wonderful little family. And I've finally worked out my situation since Daddy died. We're all together. And now old animal magnetism tries to get into the act. Well we are not going to let it interfere with your wonderful demonstration of the power of Divine Love. Your children have come to you because they were supposed to. They are literal answers to prayer, and no mortal mind thinking can interfere with God's plan for you and Barbara."

"But what the hell has brought this on?"

"Let me say something to you. Mrs. Eddy admonishes us to deny animal magnetism every day. Why does she do that? Because, in point of fact there *is no animal magnetism*," she said very distinctly. "Anytime these problems come up we must see them for what they are. No matter how real or painful they appear to be, they are not real. They are merely wayward mortal mind suggestions that have been allowed to enter our thinking and the thinking of those who have attacked us. They have nothing to do with the truth of being, and that is what we're talking about. The truth of being."

"But it's so difficult to handle these suggestions metaphysically. We're having a meeting with Mrs. Whitesill tomorrow, and we have no idea what to say or how to confront our accuser. She won't even let us know who it is."

"Listen to me carefully," my mother said. "We are not a whole bunch of little mortal minds running around on this earth, no matter how real that suggestion may seem. Each and every one of us is the full and complete expression of Divine Mind, of God. That's true for your social worker and your accuser. They are being handled by animal magnetism. But in reality, they are children of God. Remember what First John says. 'Now are we the sons of God.' *Now.* Not 'will be.'

"My suggestion to you is that you must literally see this Mrs. Whitesill as a child of God. And let God take care of the situation."

◆　　　◆　　　◆

Barbara and I sat in two straight-backed chairs across the desk from Mrs. Whitesill. Jeff had found a Fischer Price Garage, and was busily driving cars. Carly was near him playing with the Raggedy Ann doll she had brought with her.

I was struggling very hard to see Margaret in the light my mother had suggested or even as the friend I thought we knew. Barbara, however, had made it clear to me that no amount of metaphysical work could dispel her sense of animosity.

"So what can we say to straighten this business out?" I asked. "I mean here we are Margaret, our entire family. You see two reasonably well-adjusted children."

"I don't believe there is much that you can say," she responded. "We need to work out some way for you to demonstrate that the charges are untrue."

"And that would be?" Barbara spoke rather sharply. "Are we going to learn who this woman is and what has been said?"

"I am afraid that will not be possible. I had to give assurance that I would not reveal her name before she would speak to me."

Suddenly, Carly left her Raggedy Ann on the floor, walked over to Barbara, and climbed into her lap. Barbara absentmindedly put out her hand to help her up, then gently hugged her. Carly sat on Barbara's lap looking up at her and playing with Barbara's necklace. Barbara held onto the necklace to prevent Carly from pulling it too hard while she continued to speak, "I don't believe there is any way you can understand our sense of frustration. Can't you give us some clue as to where we can go from here?"

"I have given this some thought," Margaret said. "And I think the only way we can resolve this is by having a third party review the situation. I would like to hear from people who have observed you with your children. What I suggest is that you propose someone who knows you and your children who would also be qualified to speak objectively with regard to this situation. Then I would speak to them in confidence."

Silence.

Then Barbara blurted out. "You know what I can't understand? I can't understand why actions don't speak louder than words. Look at this little girl. What could be more eloquent?"

She was speaking past Carly's hand, which was reaching for her nose.

"I have to agree," I said. "What more could you ask for?" At that moment Jeff climbed up into my lap. "I mean look at these two."

"Appearances aren't enough. I need a third party opinion," Margaret said; her expression had become firm, as though she would accept no compromise.

After a moment, I let out a huge breath and said, "Okay. But I have to say something. I was hoping it wouldn't come to this. We already have been on the phone with someone who knows us and who also knows something about the adoption laws in this state. Her name is Jackie Ellis. She is my cousin-in-law. She works in Cambridge for an adoption agency. Do you know her?"

"I don't believe so," Margaret said.

"Well, the most important thing she said was that adoptive parents, even in the first year of adoption, have rights. If it becomes necessary, we will know where to go and how to exercise those rights. We will not give in to this outrageous allegation," I said as I placed Jeff on the floor and stood up. Barbara did the same with Carly.

"C'mon gang," I said.

Carly took Barbara's hand. Jeff took mine, and we left.

◆   ◆   ◆

I reported the results of our meeting in Lowell to my mother. "All right then," she responded, "let's go to work to know that the right person for this job exists now, and is known to Divine Mind, even if we don't know who it is."

We first suggested Jackie Ellis, but she was rejected because she was practically a member of our family. She couldn't possibly be objective.

More prayer.

Then my carpet-laying helper, Al Hudson, came to mind. He was training for the ministry. Part of his training involved social work. But that wasn't good enough because he wasn't experienced.

Okay.

More prayerful searching.

Finally, Jim Clark, minister at the local Baptist church came to mind. We knew him fairly well. He had had years of experience counseling his parishioners.

We also asked Jackie, Al, and several others to send letters to Margaret expressing their confidence in our parenting of Carly.

◆   ◆   ◆

Several days later, we were still waiting for Margaret Whitesill's answer regarding Rev. Clark when I called on a customer in East Gloucester. Dr. Ellen Bronstein was a psychiatrist.

We were in the process of discussing how her carpet should be installed when her phone rang. She excused herself, and then returned and said, "It's your wife."

I went to the phone, which was lying on the kitchen counter. "Hello?"

"Hello Bob." Her voice was very strained. "We've heard from Margaret Whitesill. She doesn't like Jim Clark. She doesn't think anybody we can recommend to her is going to work. They'll never be objective enough. She sounds like we could be in serious trouble. Can you come home? We need to deal with this now."

"Okay. I'll get there as quickly as I can," I said. I hung up and returned to the living room. "I'm afraid I have a serious situation at home," I said to Dr. Bronstein.

"Is there anything I can do?" she asked me.

I blurted out, "We're facing the prospect of losing our adopted daughter."

"Sit down," She said. "Tell me what's happened."

I told her everything that had transpired during the past six weeks.

"It's been hell," I ended. "We're not getting any sleep. The kids can tell something awful is going on. We're at our wit's end."

She thought silently for a moment before she said, "I don't know this Mrs. Whitesill. Nor do I know what motivated her. However, even if her motivation was proper, her actions do seem to have been unfair. Here's what occurs to me. She has forced herself into a corner by relying on you and your wife to come up with a solution to what really is her problem. She has rejected every suggestion you have made. And now she has nowhere to turn."

She paused for a second. "I suspect that she knows by now that there was no truth to the allegations. She has seen you with your children, and she has received plenty of written testimony. At this stage, however, for her to give in would be to admit that her actions have been wrong all along. But she has to do something to save face. So my suggestion would be for you to help her figure out how. Why don't you suggest that *she* find this objective third party? There are plenty of qualified people she can call upon. Let her know you trust her to do the right thing."

◆   ◆   ◆

Barbara was waiting for me as I walked in our front door. I told her about Dr. Bronstein's suggestion.

"I'm going to call Margaret, and put it all on her shoulders," I said.

I placed the call. Sounding as civil as I possibly could, I suggested to her that perhaps she could find someone whom she would consider objective. "Whichever way it goes, we will trust you to do the right thing." I could feel the tension drop away over the phone line. She thanked me and said she would get back to us.

◆   ◆   ◆

First thing the following morning, Margaret called and said she had found one Helen Morgan whom she did not know but who had an office in Cambridge. Mrs. Morgan had agreed to handle the case if we were agreeable. Without asking

Barbara, I agreed, took down Mrs. Morgan's phone number and hung up. Then I told Barbara.

"Helen Morgan?" Barbara asked. "You know our neighbor's name is Helen Morgan. She's a social worker of some kind. Do you suppose it could be the same person?"

"There's one way to find out." I picked up the phone and dialed Helen Morgan's number. She answered directly. I identified myself. We agreed on an appointment. Then she took down my address and phone number.

"I wondered if I knew you," she said. "I suppose we could meet in Rockport. But you know, given this situation, it probably would be best if we kept this as impersonal and professional as we can. So you had better come into town and meet me here."

Three days later we were sitting in Mrs. Morgan's office in Cambridge. She had suggested we not bring the children. She'd know after chatting with us if she would need to meet them. Her gentle, pleasant approach was like a breath of fresh air. There was no challenge in her voice as she asked us to relate our story. Then, as she questioned us about the past six weeks, our answers became more and more emotionally charged.

Finally after about forty-five minutes, Barbara blurted out with tears streaming down her face. "It's been so difficult, Mrs. Morgan. We love those kids so much. That anyone would think we would do anything but love them is—"

She couldn't finish her sentence.

She tried again. "Anybody who thinks that adopting an older baby is all peaches and cream is dreaming. It's hard work. Carly was thrust into our home at fourteen months of age. We didn't speak the same language. We were complete strangers to her. She was terrified. Literally. She cried and cried."

Barbara paused and stared out the window as she tried to collect her thoughts. "And her brother has been no help. All he seems to be able to do is torment her when we're not looking. We do all we can to help her, to let her know she's found a loving home. We were warned it would be like this, and we knew it intellectually. But there's no getting away from the fact that it can be unbelievably difficult. Still, slowly but surely she has started to come around. Jeff is beginning to understand that he hasn't lost our love and attention. Carly's more able to understand what is being said. She's speaking now, and showing her really delightful and at times very funny real self. It's working. It just can't be right that anyone would suggest that we should lose her." Mrs. Morgan pushed a box of Kleenex across her desk. Barbara wiped her eyes, blew her nose, and looked at the two of us with a slightly embarrassed smile on her face.

After a moment's pause, Mrs. Morgan said: "I can see no reason why it would benefit anyone involved in this situation to have your daughter removed from her home, and I will write a letter to that effect to Mrs. Whitesill. You and your family have been through quite enough."

◆   ◆   ◆

Mrs. Morgan sent us a copy of the letter she wrote to Mrs. Whitesill. When we received it, I walked to my mother's apartment and read the letter out loud to her. It was very brief and stated almost verbatim Mrs. Morgan's last words to Barbara and me.

Mother sat back with a gentle smile. "I never cease to marvel at the way Divine Intelligence operates. We work to know that only Divine Intelligence is directing us and everyone. And when we see that, then we can have the most wonderful results. Don't you for one minute believe that anything but Divine Intelligence was operating when you went to call on that customer; when Barbara called and interrupted your sales call; and when your customer overheard your conversation and showed you the way out. And who did the adoption agency come up with but your neighbor? I have to tell you, I never cease to be amazed at how it works.

◆   ◆   ◆

As Christian Scientists, Barbara and I fully understood the importance of listening to what King David called "that still small voice." I came to believe, however, that in this case we allowed ourselves to become so mesmerized by the threat of losing our daughter that God finally had to shout at us to make us hear, and Mrs. Bronstein was God's mouthpiece.

JEFF'S FOLLY

On a cold, gray Saturday morning in December 1984, the phone rang. "This is Detective John Marshall of the Gloucester Police Department. We have your son, Jeffrey, in custody. He tried to pass some bad checks at the U.S. Bank and Trust Company."

Barbara and I immediately drove to Gloucester police headquarters. We were directed to a small office where a man was sitting at a typewriter. "Come in. Have a seat. I'm Detective Marshall," he said. As we were getting ourselves seated, he said, "Your son is in the room next door. He's being fingerprinted. He'll be in here in a couple of minutes." I couldn't believe he could be speaking about our fourteen-year-old son.

"Well, what has happened?" Barbara asked in a slightly high-pitched voice.

"We got a call from the bank teller at the U.S. Bank and Trust on Railroad Avenue. She told us that a young boy claiming to be a Harold Billings, was trying to cash several checks made out to him. They totaled seven hundred and fifty dollars. I can tell you that when I saw your son, I knew we were not dealing with a hardened criminal. Even so, he *had* used a false ID for one Harold Billings, and he had an accomplice who ran away when he saw us arriving."

"But where did he get the checks?" Barbara asked. "And who's this accomplice?"

"Your son says his name is Jessie Kangas, and that Jessie found the checks in an abandoned strong box."

"Jessie?" I asked. He and Jeff were two of my Sunday school students. "What would make them think they could pass off checks totaling seven hundred and fifty dollars?" I asked.

Detective Marshall said, "I can imagine two young boys putting their heads together and thinking that maybe they could cash a check. How much? How about fifteen dollars. But if they could do fifteen dollars, why not twenty-five? And so on. The next thing they knew they were going for three checks totaling seven hundred and fifty dollars."

"So what's going to happen to him?" I asked.

"Well, he's a juvenile, so we'll release him in your custody. But I'm required by law to tell you that it'll be important for you to keep an eye on your son. What I'm talking about is the possibility of suicide. Kids Jeff's age who are under the kind of stress he's going to be experiencing, can be extremely vulnerable."

"Oh my God," Barbara exclaimed.

Detective Marshall got up, walked into the office next door, and returned with Jeff who fell into his mother's arms. "Oh, Mom," he exclaimed as he buried his face in her shoulder and clung to her. She put her arms around him, and held him tight.

"What on earth got into you, Jeff?" Barbara asked through her tears.

"I don't know Mom. I'm so sorry." He was crying. I was close to tears. But I was angry as well.

"Well, we're going to take you home now," his mother said.

Detective Marshall said. "You won't forget what I suggested?"

"No we won't. And thanks." I responded

◆　　◆　　◆

"What on earth were you two thinking?" I asked as I pulled out of the parking lot.

"I don't know, Dad."

"What do you mean you don't know? Come on, young man, you have to understand that there's no way we can help you if you don't fill us in."

"Jessie found this strongbox in Dogtown with this checkbook."

"In Dogtown!" Barbara and I echoed. Dogtown was a wilderness area full of trees and undergrowth, wild flowers, rock formations, and ancient foundations of houses that were supposedly built by colonial dwellers who had left the area and abandoned their dogs.

"Yeah. He found it a couple of weeks ago. He showed it to me last night. It was full of papers, bonds, checkbooks—all kinds of stuff."

"But what was Jessie's part in your plan to fleece the bank?"

"We didn't think we were going to fleece the bank. We just wanted to cash some checks."

"Well, where did you think the money was going to come from if not the bank?"

"I didn't mean it like that. I mean we thought the guy whose name was on the checks had an account there."

"So you were going to fleece him."

"I don't know, Dad. I mean, we didn't think—"

"You got that right," I said. "I'm still trying to understand Jessie's part in all this."

"He was the lookout."

"The lookout! So you *did* know this escapade was just a little bit shady."

As I pulled into the driveway of our home I said, "Well, young man, here's what's going to happen. We're going to go inside, and you are not leaving the house until you go to school on Monday morning. In other words, you are thoroughly grounded. Is that clear?"

"Yeah."

"We, in the meantime, are going to call Jessie's mother. I'll bet she has no idea about this. Won't she be thrilled? I wonder if Jessie's gone home."

"I think the police already found him," Jeff said. "I told them we had gone to the bank on our bikes. I heard one of them say they found a kid on his bike."

"You rode over to Gloucester to rob a bank on your *bike*?!" I exclaimed.

"We didn't try to rob a bank, Dad. Only pass some checks."

"Forged checks."

"Yeah."

"To the tune of *seven hundred and fifty dollars*!"

"Yeah."

"At the United States Bank and Trust Company!"

"Yeah."

"You can nitpick with me as much as you want, Jeffrey Scott Ellis. No matter how you look at it you were attempting some mighty powerful fleecing of a bank and/or one of its depositors," I said as we walked up the stairs and to our front door. "Down to your room, young man," I said, "and don't you even think of coming out until we say you can, except to go to the bathroom."

He went straight to his room.

I phoned Jessie's mother, Michelle. The police had arrested Jessie. He now was home with her, thoroughly grounded as well. In the meantime, Barbara and I had agreed that we needed an attorney. Michelle said that she would just as soon have our attorney represent Jessie as well.

◆   ◆   ◆

"What?! How could he? There must be some mistake!" was my mother's response when I told her about Jeff's escapade later that afternoon.

"I'm afraid there's no mistake. They caught him red-handed, so to speak."

"But you're talking about Jeffrey," she responded. My mother adored her two grandchildren.

"And Jessie Kangas."

"Jessie! Oh my. There has to be some rational explanation for this."

"The only explanation I can think of is that they are two fourteen-year-old teenagers. But, even with that, this is beyond the pale. I can't imagine how this is going to end up. I mean, Jeff could go to jail," I said.

"All right, then. Let's pull ourselves together. We have to see this as some kind of aberration. Something got hold of Jeffrey," my mother said. "We don't know what it might have been specifically. But we can name it by its real name—animal magnetism. He allowed some kind of aggressive mental suggestion to work its way into his thinking. But we know that he is literally a child of God. You know, I've always felt you and Barbara were wonderfully blessed when Jeff and Carly came into your home. That hasn't changed. We're going to have to work very, very hard to know that God is in control here. Not you. Not Barbara. Not the police or any other person. God is watching over those boys."

◆   ◆   ◆

Monday morning, our attorney Bob Mitchell agreed that he probably could represent both boys. "I'll call the police and find out what's going on," he said. Three hours later he called back. "Well, there's a lot more to this than you had reason to believe. Those checks that the boys tried to use? They belonged to a man in Rockport who, it would seem, is a known drug dealer. He claims his house was broken into and the strongbox was stolen. So now the police are wondering who stole the strongbox and how it ended up in Dogtown if indeed that is how Jessie got it, if you get my meaning. I think I had better meet with the boys ASAP, and hear their side of the story. I'll want to see them separately. How about tomorrow at 10:00 AM for Jeff?"

◆   ◆   ◆

We were awakened by the phone at almost midnight that night. "Hello, Bob. This is Harry Rosen. I'm sorry to call you at this hour, but Jane and I felt we must. Rebecca just told us that she and Jeff were on the phone." Rebecca was Harry and Jane's daughter and a classmate of Jeff's in high school. Harry continued, "Jeff swore her to secrecy, but she figured she should tell us. She said that Jeff told her he's thinking about suicide."

"Thanks, Harry. And thank Rebecca. We'll get right on it," I said.

I immediately told Barbara.

"Oh my God," she said as she leaped out of bed. We ran downstairs to Jeff's room and opened his door without knocking. He woke from a deep sleep.

"Are you all right?" Barbara asked him.

"Yeah. What's the matter?"

I didn't want to betray Rebecca's confidence. In teenager terms she had violated Jeff's trust. "It's nothing, Jeff. It's just that we felt we ought to check on you," I said.

After we left his room Barbara whispered, "What are we going to do? Shouldn't we tell him why we were checking on him?"

As we headed back upstairs I said I didn't think we should betray Rebecca to him. "Something tells me we shouldn't reinforce any ideas he may be having about suicide. Let's just make sure he's always with his schoolmates or with us."

Barbara said, "I've never been so worried in my life."

"I know. But look, we've got to know that this is animal magnetism operating. We need to deny that it has any power. We need to know that only God is present in this house. Jeff is God's perfect child. God would never let anything happen to him."

"That's easy enough to say, but I'm not sure I can stop worrying."

◆   ◆   ◆

Bob Mitchell met with Jeff for thirty minutes. Then Barbara and I joined them.

"The police have filed nine counts against him," Bob said. "So, Jeff's defense will have to be based on his overall good character. He has parents who are upstanding members of the community, he plays the violin, he practices archery, plays the trumpet, is a math whiz, speaks French, you get the drift. He's a good kid who wasn't thinking straight."

"Nine counts!?" Barbara exclaimed.

"Yes. They filed separate charges for each check. Jeff is facing three charges of forgery, three counts of attempted grand larceny because each check was greater than two hundred dollars, and three counts of utterance of a false statement—i.e., that he was Harold Billings."

"So, what can we do?" Barbara asked. "I mean this sounds very serious."

"It is. There's no getting around it. But, as I say, Jeff's never been in any trouble with the police before. So, considering everything I listed about his character, I think there's a good chance the district attorney will be reasonable."

"Is Jeff going to have to go to jail?" Barbara asked. I saw fear in Jeff's eyes.

"At this point I can't say. Possibly a youthful offender facility. If he were only one year older he definitely would be facing serious consequences."

◆   ◆   ◆

Jeff attended a small private school in Beverly where he was kept busy from 9:00 AM until 5:00 PM. When he got home he still was not allowed to leave the house, though we had allowed him out of his room. He could see none of his friends.

"I can't stand this atmosphere," Barbara finally said one morning after she returned from taking Jeff to school. I can't believe that keeping Jeff from his friends, from any social contact, can be good for him. Not when we're concerned about suicide."

"He should be grateful he's not in jail," I responded.

"Maybe so. I still can't believe this atmosphere is healthy. We need to do something. And I know he's afraid you're so angry that you don't love him anymore."

"I am angry. How can I not be angry? I would think you would be too."

"Well, yes I am. But at the same time, I'm worried. He's not a bad kid. He's made an awful mistake. But that's what it was, a mistake. We can't let him think we've given up on him. And I'm afraid he thinks you have."

"No. I haven't given up on him. If I had, we wouldn't be hiring lawyers and trying to get him out of even more serious trouble. Certainly he can see that."

"He's still a young boy, Bob. He's tremendously troubled. I don't think he's able to think things through so logically. You're his father, and he needs your love."

"Well he should be troubled, damn it! How could he not be troubled? I mean, I never dreamed my son could be so stupid. Where's the kid I thought I knew? He was always doing silly things. But they were just that; they were silly and funny. But this, this is beyond me."

"Bob, he's never again going to be that sweet little fellow he once was. He's becoming a young man now. And right now he needs our love more than ever."

"I know you're right, Barbara. I really do. And I do love him. You know that."

"Of course I know you love him. But does he? That's my concern."

"Well what can I do?" I asked.

"For starters, you can tell him. And it also might make sense for you to get him out of this house. Give him some kind of reprieve from this prison we've put him in."

"Where would I take him?"

"How about skiing? Take him this weekend—just the two of you. Carly and I will be just fine this weekend with you two away. In fact, I'm sure it'll be a relief to her. The tension in this house is so thick you could cut it with a knife."

◆   ◆   ◆

That following Friday night Jeff and I arrived at the Christmas Farm Inn in Jackson, New Hampshire. "Well, Jeff," I said as we sat at dinner, "It's been a hell of a week, hasn't it?"

"Yeah."

"What do you say we try to put it all behind us for now? Let's try to just have some fun. Do you think that'll work?"

"I guess so," he answered.

"Look, Jeff. I know I've been pretty hard on you this week. But I honestly don't believe I've overreacted. What you and Jessie tried to pull off was absolutely beyond comprehension. But it doesn't change the fact that I only want what's best for you. It doesn't change the fact that I love you. Can you understand that?"

"Yeah. I think so."

"Well then. Can we do as I've suggested? Can we let go of everything and just do some good downhill? Let's enjoy ourselves and let the future take care of itself."

"Okay, Dad. I'll try."

The following day we skied Attatash. Jeff was a better skier than I. He was much faster, much more bold, and always challenging me to beat him to the bottom of the hill. As the day progressed we both became much more like our old selves. On the chairlift it started to snow very lightly. Jeff looked at his black mittens, which were resting on the safety bar. "Look Dad," he said as he pointed to the mittens. Snowflakes were landing on his mitten as individual crystals.

"That is something," I said. "Supposedly no two are alike in the entire universe. The number of designs is infinite. Makes you wonder, doesn't it?"

"Yeah, I know. I've heard about it. But this is the first time I've actually seen them. Look how they just rest on my mitten. And it's true. No two are alike." He looked at me with a gentle smile on his face. I was seeing my normal son again.

◆ ◆ ◆

At dinner that night we were very tired and wonderfully relaxed. I now found myself able to broach the subject that couldn't help but be on our minds.

"You know what I don't understand, Jeff? I can't understand how in the world you talked yourself into trying to pass those checks. I know everyone will tell me that it's because of your age and all that kind of stuff. But I don't buy it."

"Jessie had some vodka in his hideout in back of his house. He has all kinds of stuff out there. That's where he showed me the strongbox and the checkbook."

"Did you say vodka?" This was my underage Christian Science Sunday school student and son telling me he had been drinking vodka. Christian Scientists do not drink alcohol of any kind. Not ever. "You and Jessie drank vodka?"

"Yeah. Half a bottle. We weren't thinking too clearly. I spent the night there, you know. The next morning, I wasn't feeling too good. That was when we biked to the bank."

"My God, Jeff!" I paused. Then I asked, "Okay, then. While we're having true confessions, can you tell me how you ever thought you were going to explain having seven hundred and fifty dollars worth of checks in your pocket?"

"I was going to say I had been paid for lawn mowing jobs."

"Lawn mowing jobs? In December?" I couldn't help but smile.

◆ ◆ ◆

On a cold, January day, I walked into Jeff's room. He lay in his bed, flat on his back, stiff as a board, his eyes staring at the ceiling. "How are you doing?" I asked.

His eyes shifted to me, "I'm really scared, Dad."

I said, "I know you are, but you have to go through this. You know that." Then I heard myself saying, "You know, Jeff, I have often wondered why Mom and I had to wait nine years to have a child, and the reason came to me last night. Can you imagine what it is?"

"No."

"It was because *we were waiting for you.*"

His eyes widened into saucers.

"Well. You had better get up. We have to be in court by 9:00 AM. We'll be with you. We sure don't like what you did, but that doesn't change the fact that we love you."

◆   ◆   ◆

At 8:45 AM we entered the Gloucester courthouse. There we found Jessie, his mother, his stepfather, and Bob Mitchell. The District Attorney had not yet arrived. Bob told us to have a seat. He would come get us as soon as all the participants had assembled.

Soon he returned and said, "They're ready." We followed him into a large, windowless room behind the main courtroom. We were seated at a long conference table. Several people I did not recognize sat along one side. Barbara, myself, Jeff, Jessie, his stepfather, Michelle, and Bob Mitchell sat at the end and up the other side. As soon as we were seated, Judge Harold Lumbard came in. He was dressed in his robes even though this was not the courtroom.

"All right. What do we have here?" he asked the clerk of the court.

"This is the matter of the Commonwealth of Massachusetts vs. Jeffrey Ellis and Jessie Kangas, your honor."

"Ah yes," he said as he turned to the District Attorney. "Proceed, please, Mr. Landry."

"Your Honor, on Saturday morning, December 13, 1984, Jeffrey Ellis attempted to pass three forged checks all in amounts greater than two hundred dollars and totaling seven hundred and fifty dollars at the United States Bank and Trust Company on Railroad Avenue in Gloucester. Jessie Kangas stood outside the bank as a lookout while Mr. Ellis attempted the transaction. The bank teller called the police, and they arrested Mr. Ellis. Shortly thereafter, Mr. Kangas was arrested. It was determined by both the Rockport and Gloucester Police that the checks had been found by Mr. Kangas in a strongbox, which had been discarded in Dogtown after it had been stolen from a home in Rockport."

Jeff was white as a sheet. He had to be wondering where these formal proceedings were headed. Would Judge Lumbard send these boys to a juvenile detention center? I, too, wondered even though Bob had said everything probably would be okay.

"What are your recommendations?" Judge Lumbard asked the DA.

"Your honor, this was a first offence for both boys. Both are presently in the custody of their parents who are here this morning. They are full-time students, Mr. Kangas in the Rockport Schools and Mr. Ellis at the Waring School in Beverly. Their school records indicate that they are good students. Mr. Mitchell has assured us that the defendants will never engage in any illegal acts in the future. Therefore, the Commonwealth recommends that the defendants be given probation for six months, and that they be released in the custody of their parents. And that, if after six months there has been no further illegal activity on their part, their records in this matter be sealed."

"Mr. Mitchell?"

"The parents agree to everything the District Attorney has outlined, your honor."

"All right then young men," Judge Lumbard said as he looked at Jeff and Jessie. "I have been given assurances by the District Attorney, Mr. Mitchell, and by your parents that you will never again involve yourselves in any illegal acts. I have been assured that this behavior of yours was an aberration, that you are normally well behaved, well-adjusted young men. Since the District Attorney has recommended that you be released in your parents' custody and on six months probation, I am willing to entertain that resolution. Let me say this to you, however. If I ever see you gentlemen in this courtroom again, I will throw the book at you. Is that understood?" His eyes bore into Jessie's and Jeff's eyes."

"Yes sir," they both responded.

"Then it is so ordered," he said before he rose from his chair and left the room.

◆　　◆　　◆

We left the courthouse and drove in silence to Jeff's school. I stared at his back as he walked into the administration building. "There is no way I could love that young man more than I do. But how do you explain it?" I asked. "The sacrifices and the incredible angst we accept? Why do we do it?"

"Because we can't help loving our children," Barbara answered.

◆　　◆　　◆

I asked my mother the same question when I reported the court room proceedings to her later that day.

"It's a question I've asked myself from time to time." She said. "And I have no pat answer. One does have to wonder how parents can stand some of the agonies that they can be put through. I'm thinking not only of strange behavior. Just think of what it must be like to have a child come down with cancer or to lose a child. I cannot fathom what that would be like. Yes, we have our understanding in Christian Science, and it carries us through these ordeals. But—?" She was staring off into space. Then she focused on me and smiled, "Well. At least in this instance we can only be grateful. You, Barbara, and your children have been beautifully protected."

◆   ◆   ◆

It was my turn to pick up Jeff from school that afternoon. "Hi, Dad," he said as he hopped in the car. He was his bright and cheerful self once again. Two other classmates hopped in as well. It was my turn to deliver them to their parents.

"Thank you, Father," I said to myself as I listened to Jeff and his classmates chatting among themselves. "Thank you for giving me back my son."

LUX ETERNA

On the last Sunday morning in January 1989, I was the first to arrive at First Church of Christ, Scientist, Rockport. I was scheduled to substitute as First Reader. I walked the length of the small auditorium, stepped up onto the platform, and checked my books. Nancy, the regular Second Reader, and I had rehearsed the service the previous evening. I now made certain one more time that everything was in order.

The front door opened, and in came Jim Henderson. "Hello, Bob," he said.

"Hi, Jim," I returned.

Jim was head usher. He was there to make certain that everything was in order in the front of the church. Were the collection bags in their proper places? Were the Quarterlies correctly located for ushers to hand out to the congregants as they came in? Were the hymnals properly placed in the backs of the pews?

As he started his routine, I left the platform and headed toward the back of the building. Just as I was closing the door to the First Reader's office, I heard Nancy coming in and greeting Jim.

I had about twenty minutes before it would be time to start the service. These minutes prior to going out always were, for me, a time to be quiet. I had studied the readings thoroughly. Nancy and I had rehearsed them. So I was intellectually prepared. I reminded myself of David's admonition, "Be still and know that I am God."

"Okay God. This is your service. It's out of my hands," I said quietly. As I leaned back in my chair and closed my eyes, I fell into another special, meditative moment. My surroundings seemed to disappear. All was very peaceful, very quiet. I felt a palpable presence surrounding me, even warming me. I felt completely at one with God.

Soon, the bass tones of the organ rumbled the walls. It was nearing time to step out and join Nancy at the door to the platform. We would wait until one minute before 10:00 AM; then we would step out, walk to our chairs, and sit down behind the podium.

I heard Nancy coming out of her office. It was time to join her. She smiled a greeting to me as we both approached the door. Jim Henderson had appointed himself the usher who would open the door for us. I checked my watch. The second hand was approaching one minute before ten. Jim opened the door. The three of us filed out. Nancy and I went to our chairs on the platform and sat down. Jim closed the door behind him and went to a seat in the front pew. The organ prelude ended. The sense of peace remained with me as I rose, stepped toward the desk, and said, "Good morning."

Suddenly an inexplicable sensation of golden light bathed the auditorium. Everybody and everything was included in it. It was like when the sun sets behind us and everything is covered in gold. But this was much more brilliant, even otherworldly. I was amazed but not surprised. I had carried with me that sense of peace that had descended upon me in my office. I had never had such an experience before. But I had heard of others who had. "So, this is what they're talking about," I thought to myself.

Finally, I started the service. "Let us sing hymn No. 207. The words of this hymn are by the discoverer and founder of Christian Science, Mary Baker Eddy." Traditionally, every Sunday service should include a hymn by Mrs. Eddy, except on the third Sunday of the month when the soloist sang one of Mrs. Eddy's poems, which would be set to music different from the hymnal's settings.

I sat down, and the organist played the hymn through once. Then we all rose and sang. I looked at Barbara who sat next to my mother in the center section of pews, three rows in from the rear. She knew the hymn by heart, as did most of those present, so she was looking up as I glanced at her. She gave me a quick smile.

I remained standing while Nancy and the congregation sat down after the hymn. I announced, "The Scriptural selection is from First John." The verses ended with, "And we have known and believed the love that God hath to us. God is love; and he that dwelleth in love dwelleth in God, and God in him."[1]

As I closed my Bible and inserted it on the shelf underneath the desk, Nancy rose from her chair to stand beside me while I said, "Let us have a moment of silent prayer, then follow by saying the Lord's Prayer with its spiritual interpretation found in the Christian Science textbook." We all bowed our heads.

After about a minute, Nancy said, "Our Father, which art in heaven." The congregation joined in; then stopped as I read Mrs. Eddy's spiritual interpretation of that line. "Our Father-Mother God, all-harmonious." Then Nancy and the congregation continued reciting while I interjected the spiritual interpretation of each line.[2]

---

1.   I John 4:16

After we finished the prayer, I called upon the congregation to sing another hymn. Then I read the announcements and sat down.

The soprano soloist who was sitting in the front pew, rose and sang her solo. After she sat down, I rose from my chair, and read the following announcement, which Mrs. Eddy composed for every service and which appears in the first pages of the *Quarterly*:

> Friends, the Bible and the Christian Science textbook, are our only preachers. We shall now read Scriptural texts, and their correlative passages from our denominational textbook. These comprise our sermon;
>
> The canonical writings together with the word of our textbook, corroborating and explaining the Bible texts in their spiritual import and application to all ages, past, present, and future, constitute a sermon undivorced from Truth, uncontaminated and unfettered by human hypotheses, and divinely authorized.

I looked up at the congregation and said, "The lesson sermon for today begins on page thirty of the *Christian Science Quarterly*." Most everyone already had their *Quarterly* open. But a few quickly flipped their pages to today's lesson/sermon.

---

2.   The complete prayer with its spiritual interpretation is found in *S&H*, Page 16 starting on line 26. It reads:
> Our Father which art in heaven,
> Our Father-Mother God, all-harmonious,
> Hallowed be Thy name.
> Adorable One.
> Thy kingdom come.
> Thy kingdom is come; Thou art ever-present.
> Thy will be done in earth, as it is in heaven.
> Enable us to know,—as in heaven, so on earth,—God is omnipotent, supreme.
> Give us this day our daily bread;
> Give us grace for today; feed the famished affections;
> And forgive us our debts, as we forgive our debtors.
> And Love is reflected in love.
> And lead us not into temptation, but deliver us from evil;
> And God leadeth us not into temptation, but delivereth us from sin, disease, and death.
> For Thine is the kingdom, and the power, and the glory, forever.
> For God is infinite, all-power, all Life, Truth, Love, over all, and All.

"Subject: Love."[3] I paused briefly, then said, "The Golden Text is from Zephaniah: 'The Lord thy God in the midst of thee is mighty; he will save, he will rejoice over thee with joy; he will rest in his love, he will joy over thee with singing.'"[4]

I continued: "The Responsive Readings are from First Corinthians." I read the first verse. The congregation joined Nancy in reading the second verse. We continued in this fashion through the eight verses that the Lesson Committee in Boston had chosen.

After the Responsive Reading Nancy announced "the Bible" and read the three selections from the first of six sections listed in the *Quarterly*.

I followed by saying: "As announced in the explanatory note, I shall now read correlative passages from the Christian Science textbook, *Science and Health with Key to the Scriptures* by Mary Baker Eddy." I then read the four citations listed in the first section. Then Nancy followed by reading Bible citations in the next section. I followed with the *Science and Health* citations, and we continued alternating in this manner until we had completed all six sections.

We sat down. The organist played while the ushers passed the collection bags. We used bags so that people would not be able to see what their neighbor had donated.

When the ushers finished, I stood up and announced the third hymn. After we finished singing, Nancy, the congregation and I remained standing and I announced, "I shall now read the scientific statement of being from the Christian Science textbook:"

> There is no life, truth, intelligence, nor substance in matter. All is infinite Mind and its infinite manifestation, for God is All-in-all. Spirit is immortal Truth; matter is mortal error. Spirit is the real and eternal; matter is the unreal and temporal. Spirit is God, and man is His image and likeness. Therefore man is not material; he is spiritual.[5]

---

3.   Mrs. Eddy prescribed twenty-six lesson subjects to be studied twice each year. They are: God; Sacrament; Life; Truth; Love; Spirit; Soul; Mind; Christ Jesus; Man; Substance; Matter; Reality; Unreality; Are Sin, Disease, and Death Real?; Doctrine of Atonement; Probation After Death; Everlasting Punishment; Adam and Fallen Man; Mortals and Immortals; Soul and Body; Ancient and Modern Necromancy, *alias* Mesmerism and Hypnotism, Denounced; God the Only Cause and Creator; God the Preserver of Man; Is the Universe, Including Man, Evolved by Atomic Force?; Christian Science. Also a Thanksgiving service is published annually in November and is modeled after a Wednesday Meeting.

4.   Zephaniah 3:17

I continued: "And the correlative passage from the Bible, First John, third chapter:"

> Behold, what manner of love the Father hath bestowed upon us, that we should be called the sons of God: therefore the world knoweth us not, because it knew him not. Beloved, now are we the sons of God, and it doth not yet appear what we shall be: but we know that, when he shall appear, we shall be like him; for we shall see him as he is. And every man that hath this hope in him purifieth himself, even as he is pure.[6]

These were required readings. However the benediction was to be chosen by the First Reader. I paused for a second, then turned to Jude in the New Testament and read, "Keep yourselves in the love of God."[7] I then said, "Amen." Many of the congregation remained seated while the organist played the postlude.

◆   ◆   ◆

Barbara and my mother returned home immediately after the service. I followed five or ten minutes later after gathering up all my belongings. I placed my attaché case full of my books inside the front door, removed my heavy coat, and went up to my mother's room. She had moved into a suite we had built for her in our home about a year ago after her landlord decided he needed her apartment for his family.

"What did you think?" I asked Mother as I walked into her room. She was sitting in her high-backed armchair.

"There was something very different about today's service. It's hard to put my finger on it. It was as though the atmosphere in the place was transformed," my mother said.

"You know," I said. "I usually receive a few compliments from folks after each service. But I'd have to say they were different this time. Margie said the same as you. And a couple of others spoke to me similarly. Penny told me she got some answers she'd been seeking. She felt she had been healed. She didn't say of what. But—"

---

5.   *S&H* 468:9
6.   John 3: 1–3
7.   Jude 1:21

"Well it was quite remarkable, Bob. A truly healing service. You know I wouldn't say so if I didn't believe it. I wonder what brought it about? I know you always study carefully before each service. But, as I say, this was quite different."

"Something did happen today." I said after a pause. "I didn't think I'd be able to tell anybody about it. But—"

"What was it?"

I told her about the light, then said, "I've never experienced anything like it before. Does it make any sense?"

"Oh, yes. You're not the first to have such an experience. But you must have been doing some powerful mental work before the service."

"I did pray, of course. But no more than usual. Though, just before coming out, I said, 'Okay, God, it's in your hands.' And I did feel a sense of peace descend on me. I felt as though I no longer was conducting the service. Can you understand that?"

"That could be what did it."

"Have you ever had a similar experience?"

"Not in church," she said before she paused slightly, "I've never told anybody else this, but on the night Daddy was killed, I believe I saw the same light."

"You did?" I must have sounded a bit incredulous.

"Yes. It was quite wonderful. Before I went home that evening I stopped at the A&P over on Broadway to shop for some things for our dinner. As I was standing there wondering what to buy, suddenly a brilliant, gold light filled the place. Just as you said, everybody and everything was covered in that light. I'm sure it was only with me. I don't believe another soul noticed it. And, like you, I felt a sudden sense of peace. As if I was being assured, even cared for, in some way." She paused briefly, then said: "So you can see why I wasn't surprised at what you told me. Something extraordinary did happen in that church this morning."

"My God, Mother. When was this?"

"It was about 6:30 that night."

"That's the time they said Dad was killed."

"I know."

"But what was it, Mother?"

"I can only tell you, Bob, that I have known of others who have had similar experiences, always involving that golden light. And it often changes them. I wonder if your experience will change you. Whatever happens I don't believe it makes sense to try to analyze these things. Not from any human perspective. You had the experience. It blessed everyone in that church. Accept it. And I wouldn't discuss it with anyone else except Barbara. At least not until you have made it your own. Maybe sometime later you'll share it with others—others who will understand and benefit."

I suddenly thought back to my twentieth college reunion and that lecture about the wonders of the cosmos. I had started studying after that lecture. Much of what I read was rather tough sledding, especially in the fields of relativity and quantum theory. One thing became clear, however. According to these twentieth century descriptions of the physical world, absolutely nothing is as it seems. Our three-dimensional view of the world deceives us. Not unlike a Christian Science perspective, it seemed to me.

I also consumed Carl Jung's autobiography and several other books related to his conclusions. Jung identified the numinous side of human existence as being every bit as important to our understanding of our existence as is the purely physical side. Within this numinous side exists the golden light. I read descriptions by mostly deeply religious people but also so-called common folk who, down through the ages, had experienced something similar to what I believed I had experienced that morning.

My mother always maintained that the complete description of "the truth of being" was contained in Mary Baker Eddy's writings. At the same time, however, after she heard the story of my twentieth reunion she handed me one of the first of many books that would introduce me to the world of twentieth century physics and psychology.

"So what is going on here?" I now asked myself. "Will I find an answer? Can any human explanation ever satisfy? Perhaps Mother's right. Perhaps I should just accept this experience. But how can I not wonder? What is this power we call God, which can illumine the world the way it did for me this morning?"

IN-LAWS

In the middle of May 1992, my mother-in-law collapsed in the lobby of the Ralph Waldo Emerson Inn, which my in-laws also owned. The Emerson was a half mile down the street from the Yankee Clipper. She explained to Barbara, "I seem to get out of breath very quickly. I'm sure it's just some temporary problem. I've called Betty." Betty was her practitioner.

Two weeks earlier we had met my in-laws at Boston's Logan Airport upon their return from their winter home in Sarasota, Florida. Both had startled us by arriving in wheelchairs. They said that they were tired and wanted to escape the long walk from the plane to the baggage area. Dad also said he was suffering from a painful ailment in his legs.

The following day, my mother-in-law announced that she and her husband had decided to temporarily move into a ground floor suite at the Emerson. "Everything will be on one floor. And the staff will be able to help us. One more thing. We want to rent a wheelchair for Poppa. And while we're at it, why not one for me?"

◆　　　◆　　　◆

At 2:00 AM on May 31, my mother-in-law phoned from the Emerson. "Can I speak with Barbara?" she asked.

Barbara pulled herself up from under the covers and took the phone. "Hello Mother … Oh dear … All right. We'll be right there." She hung up and said: "Daddy's calling out in pain. He wants to go to the hospital. Mother wants us to come over. She's phoning Betty."

We arrived at my in-laws' room by about 2:15 AM. My father-in-law was thrashing about on his bed in extreme pain. "What shall I do?" Barbara's mother asked. "Betty's working for him. But you can see he's not responding. I've called 911."

A patrol car arrived followed by an ambulance. Two paramedics sized up the situation very quickly, brought in a gurney, and got Dad into the ambulance.

150

They left with lights blinking but no siren. The streets of Rockport were very quiet.

Barbara and her mother followed the ambulance to the hospital. I returned home.

I lay in bed staring at the ceiling. Our house had many skylights and the sliding glass doors were open to the ocean breezes. Moonlight was pouring in. I could see a spider slowly working its way across the ceiling. The sea was very still. Small waves reflected the moonlight. Straitsmouth lighthouse blinked its regular signal. Clearly the world had no idea of the turmoil that was going on in my thoughts. Have we all failed as Christian Scientists?

How can this be? He's eighty-two. My mother's ninety and seemingly indestructible. It just doesn't seem right. He's always been so vital, so full of energy, so loyal to his church.

As we were driving over to the Emerson, Barbara had said, "Somehow you never expect that your parents will die. I know it's a childish thought. But they're your parents. Parents don't die!"

◆　　　◆　　　◆

Barbara moved over to the Emerson to stay with her mother. She had to help her get to the bathroom and to dress. And my mother-in-law was completely confined to her wheelchair. Barbara wheeled her to the dining room for her meals. She wheeled her out to the car for their daily journey to the hospital. Barbara wheeled her from the car to her dad's hospital room. Barbara's mother, for the most part, could not take more than one or two steps at a time without becoming short of breath.

Dad was hooked up to various tubes, but he was coherent when I visited him the following day. He was exhausted but managed to smile. It was obvious that the hospital staff were taking good care of him. Most importantly, he was no longer in such pain.

That afternoon, a doctor came into the waiting room where Barbara and her mother were sitting while Dad was sleeping. "Your husband is very sick. We're having a specialist look at him. He'll be here later today," he said. The man was very curt, even rude. Barbara later told me she wondered if he had spoken as he did because her father was a Christian Scientist and had not been in a hospital nor seen a doctor for most of his adult life.

Around four o'clock that afternoon my mother and I found Barbara and her mother in the waiting room. We had just looked in on Dad; he seemed comfortable and asleep. "I can't stand watching Dad with all those tubes attached to him," Barbara said. "So when he's asleep we come in here." She was working a jigsaw puzzle. Her mother was leaning back in her wheelchair. She had been dozing a bit.

We sat down. Mother sat next to my mother-in-law and took her hand. They smiled at each other. My mother and my in-laws had become close friends since Mother had moved to Rockport. While my in-laws had their own practitioner who was in Sarasota, they often consulted with Mother. And she seemed to me to be a very helpful presence at this instant. While she had not had the need of a doctor or hospital thus far, she had visited many of her patients who had been admitted to a hospital. She had brought them comfort, a sense of God's loving care. In a way she was doing the same here.

A man came into the waiting room, "Mrs. Wemyss?"

"Yes," my mother-in-law answered.

"I'm Doctor Levin. I've talked with your husband and told him that he has cancer of the liver. I'm afraid it's not curable."

"You told him??!!"

"Well ... yes."

"Oh my God!" my mother-in-law declared.

"Do you have any prognosis?" I asked the doctor.

"It's hard to say, but he probably doesn't have very long to live—a week or two. He's in great pain, as you know. So he's being given morphine via the IV. It keeps him comfortable. But it does make him very sleepy. As the days go on he'll probably need an increase in the dosage. There's nothing much else we can do for him."

The four of us went into Dad's room with Barbara pushing her mother's chair. Dad was awake but his eyes were slightly closed. Barbara pushed her mother's wheelchair next to the bed. My mother sat on the other side and this time took Dad's hand. Barbara and I stood at the foot of the bed.

Dad slowly looked at the four of us. Then his eyes settled on my mother.

"How are you feeling, Fred?" she asked him.

"Very tired. It's this medicine they're giving me for the pain. It's hard to concentrate. Have they told you?"

"Yes they have. Now listen to me, Fred. I'm not going to give you a whole bunch of Christian Science platitudes. Only this; these people in this hospital are giving you the best care they can. We can be grateful for that. But we also can be grateful that you are in God's care. Love is caring for you right now, loving you, embracing you, holding you. And you need to know that we all love you very dearly as well. We're here with you and will remain with you. No man has ever been more loved than you are right now." She got up, leaned over, and kissed him on his forehead.

Dad smiled. "Thank you Katherine."

◆   ◆   ◆

At 1:00 PM on Saturday, June 13, 1992, Dad passed away. His wife was alone in the room with him.

A nurse told Barbara. "In a way you can be grateful. My grandfather had liver cancer diagnosed early on. He spent two years going through hell. At least your father was able to lead a relatively normal life until the last few weeks."

"So was he in some way blessed?" I asked Barbara.

"Who knows?" she said as great tears poured down her cheeks.

◆   ◆   ◆

The following Tuesday morning we were getting ready to attend the funeral at 11:00 AM at the Burgess and Mackey Funeral Home on upper Main Street in Rockport. Carly, who was a senior, had returned home from boarding school and Jeff, now in his last year of art school, from New York. They wanted to see their Poppa one last time before he died. Barbara had remained with her mother at the Emerson.

The phone rang. It was Barbara sounding frantic.

"Bob. Come over here right away. Mother's collapsed!"

As I hung up the phone, I heard the fire horn blast three times calling for an ambulance. Soon after, I heard sirens. I arrived at the Emerson to find the ambulance parked in the middle of the street with its lights blinking. A patrol car was behind it. I pulled into the Emerson's parking lot and ran to my mother-in-law's room. Barbara's brother Gary, who was the manager of the Emerson, had his mother on the floor, and was administering CPR. He was a member of the volunteer fire department. Paramedics, police, Barbara, and I filled the room. Soon, Gary got his mother breathing again. She was lifted onto a gurney, and taken out to the ambulance. One of the paramedics said to Gary, "You did all you could." Gary had a bleak look on his face.

The ambulance left with sirens screaming.

Barbara came over to me. "I've never felt so helpless in my life," she said.

"Me too," I said. "But what happened?"

"I was helping Mother get dressed for the funeral. Suddenly she stopped, looked at me and said, 'I can't go through with this.' I said, 'Of course you can, Mother. You have to. It's Daddy's funeral.' Then she collapsed.

"She said, 'I'm dying.' I told her, 'You can't die, Mother. Not now,' and then I called Gary. He was just outside."

"Jesus. Is she going to be okay?" I asked.

"I don't know. You know, Bob, she has congestive heart failure, and she's refused to go into the hospital for it."

"I didn't know that."

"It's true. I saw the symptoms on a poster on the wall at the hospital, just outside Daddy's room. She had all of them—shortness of breath, swollen ankles, all of it. The doctor asked her about it, and she only agreed to take some medicine he prescribed. He wanted her to go into the hospital, but she refused."

My mother-in-law died in the ambulance. When the hospital told us, we all looked at each other disbelievingly. "I can't believe it." Barbara said. "Mom and Dad are gone. Just like that. Gone!"

◆   ◆   ◆

We had to cancel Dad's funeral. People had started arriving when we phoned the funeral director. He had to turn everyone away. "I've never had this happen before," he told us. "Never. And I've been in the business a long time."

◆   ◆   ◆

Three days later the funeral home was packed with members of the church, fellow innkeepers, members of the chamber of commerce, neighbors, and friends. I don't believe my in-laws had any idea how many people were fond of them and respected them. It was wonderfully gratifying to see and shake hands with so many folks.

Several days later we had a burial service at the Locust Grove Cemetery on the edge of town. Barbara had had a stone erected with my in-laws names on it. And the United States Army had presented a plaque commemorating my father-in-law's service as a Captain in France and Germany during the Second World War. My in-laws had been cremated. Barbara and Gary placed the urns in the ground.

We stood in a circle, holding hands as we recited the Twenty-third Psalm. As we recited, I found myself looking up at the deep blue sky. The moon was visible even though it was bright daylight. There were no clouds. I thought about my mother, who every now and then would say to me, "I wonder what Daddy's thinking right now." Were my in-laws somehow present here, thinking? Was my father? I had just finished reading a book by two quantum theorists in which the authors speculated that a connectedness exists amongst all entities in the universe, possibly revealing a conscious universe.[1] We, therefore, are inexorably connected to the universe and to all people over all time. Christian Science has it that life is eternal. In reality there is no death. Not of the real person. Not of the child of God. Mrs. Eddy says that man "coexists with God and the universe."[2]

"Are we still connected? My in-laws? My father?" I wondered silently. I looked at my mother. She looked toward me and smiled gently. "She'll be next. I wonder what her circumstances will be? I expect one day, hopefully way in the future, I'll find her sitting in her favorite chair with her books in her lap apparently asleep." I returned her smile with what may have seemed like a rather wry expression, then looked toward the ocean, which was visible through the trees.

"What is going on?" I asked myself. "My father died under the gloomiest of circumstances and surroundings. My in-laws died suddenly but basically at the top of their form in their chosen business. And, so what? What is the point? It's all very well to declare that life is eternal. That we coexist with God. But, as I look at those two holes in the ground with those urns in them—!"

---

1. *The Conscious Universe* by Menas Kafatos and Robert Nadeau. 1990 Springer-Verlag New York, Inc.
2. *S&H* 266:29

CYCLOTRON

In the late fall of 1993 my mother complained of a "strange problem" in her left eye. She agreed she ought to have her eyes examined. Perhaps her prescription needed adjusting.

After examining my mother, the ophthalmologist came into the waiting room. "Mr. Ellis, we have to talk. Your mother has a tumor in her left eye. The normal procedure in these cases is to remove the eye in order to prevent any spread of the cancer. And very soon."

Remove Mother's eye! I couldn't imagine it. "Have you told her?"

"No."

"How about removing the tumor?"

He thought for a moment, then said there was a specialist in Boston who might be able to remove the tumor.

The next day, Mother and I went to Massachusetts Eye and Ear Infirmary, a many-storied building connected to the huge complex that is Massachusetts General Hospital on the edge of the Charles River in Boston. We took the elevator to the sixth floor.

Mother stared off into space presumably knowing the truth while we sat in the waiting room.

As I sat there, I couldn't help wonder about the fact that we seemed to be spending a lot of time in hospitals. The death of my in-laws brought us to the hospital. Immediately after their death, Barbara, suffered from a detached retina, which brought us to this same hospital for successful treatment. About a year ago, Mother experienced serious bleeding. Barbara insisted she visit a gynecologist. She was immediately operated on. A huge cancerous growth was successfully removed. Now we were asking the medical profession to help with yet another ailment.

"But," I thought to myself, "Christian Science calls for 'radical reliance' on God for all healing. So how do you rationalize this? I suppose I can't. We are daily confronted with the wonders of medicine. I was taught that the medical message is insidiously working its way into our consciousness such that we no longer fully trust God. Are Mother and I and our family being taken in by medicine?"

I didn't know. At least for now I didn't care. I only hoped our visit here would be successful.

Mother's name was called. We were led into an examining room. After putting some drops in Mother's eye, a young woman had Mother look into a machine. She looked at mother's eye from the other side. Then she went to a desk, and drew a picture. She went back and forth from Mother to the desk as she refined her picture. Finally she asked us to wait. I felt I was becoming an old hand at this. I had witnessed the same procedure when they examined Barbara for her detached retina.

Soon, Dr. Nicholas Dixon came in. He conferred with the first doctor, looked at her hand-drawn picture, then had mother stare into the machine. He studied Mother's eye for quite some time, talked to the other doctor, suggested refinements in the drawing. Finally, he said, "Okay Mrs. Ellis. You can relax. You do have a tumor. It needs to be taken care of right away. Fortunately, it's been caught in time, and it is treatable. Shall I tell you what we will have to do?"

"Yes, please," Mom said.

"We'll be using the cyclotron over at Harvard to aim a beam of protons at the tumor. But here's the thing. We have to be certain that the beam attacks only the tumor and not any other part of the eye. So we're going to have to take many photographs of your eye to determine the exact size and outline of the tumor. You can imagine that it is not a perfect circle. Rather, it's like a small island in a lake with many little coves and harbors. What we will do is craft a small bronze ring, the inside circle of which exactly matches the tumor in size and contours. When you go to Harvard and they point the gun at your eye, the ring will only allow radiation that exactly matches the contours of the tumor.

"We also will need to construct a mask that will protect your entire face including your other eye from any radiation. So you'll need to have your face measured for that purpose. I know it sounds like a complicated procedure. But it does work, and I'm pretty certain we will be successful. We've done it many times. We'll take the first set of photos today. You're going to have a week or ten days of some pretty intensive examination. Then we'll send you over to Harvard."

"Thank you," Mother said.

"You're welcome."

We returned to the waiting room.

Soon we heard, "Katherine Ellis?" The young lady at the reception desk directed us down the lengthy hall to another office complex. There were eight procedures that had to be completed today. I never was certain what they were except that each required mother to expose her left eye to various machines. Finally, at about 3:00 PM, we were done.

We made four more trips to Boston. These were gruelingly fatiguing days for Mother. Each time we returned home, she went to bed for a nap. Finally, on the last day, Dr. Dixon announced that they were ready to send her across the Charles River to the cyclotron on Oxford Street in Cambridge. Our appointment would be at 10:00 AM in two days. The brass ring and the mask would be waiting for us there. Mother would have to make a total of five weekly trips to Harvard.

On a very cold January morning in 1994, Mother and I drove to Harvard University. The cyclotron was in a small one-story, flat-roofed building, which was tucked behind other much more grand Harvard buildings. We opened the front, wood-paneled door, and found ourselves in a small Spartan waiting area where other patients were seated on metal folding chairs. We checked in with a receptionist who had us take a seat.

Soon Mother's name was called, and we were directed to the nether regions of the building via a labyrinth of halls. We entered a large interior hall in which a dentist-type chair sat. Mounted on the chair where there should have been a headrest was a metal apparatus with a large steel ring, which looked like it went around a person's head. The chair was fastened to the floor and was facing a small window. Inside the window, I saw what appeared to be the end of a small-caliber cannon.

We found a small office in which sat a young man and a woman, each dressed in a white laboratory coat. As we approached, the woman rose from her chair and came out to greet us. "Mrs. Ellis?"

"Yes."

"Welcome to the Harvard Cyclotron Laboratory. We're ready for you. We can get right to work. I'm Iris Goldman and this is Jack Grogan," she said indicating the young man.

He rose from his seat, smiled at Mother and me and said, "Hi."

I introduced myself, and Iris pointed me toward a folding chair that faced the chair where Mother would be sitting.

"Okay, Mrs. Ellis, I have to ask you to sit in this chair. It's a dentist's chair that we've modified for this procedure."

"All right, dear," Mom said. She then climbed into the chair.

"Now before we shoot your eye with a bunch of protons, we need to be certain that we are aiming them accurately. In a moment I'll ask you to rest your chin on this cup." A plastic chin-shaped cup extended down from the apparatus that held the ring.

"Then I am going to tighten this ring around your head and lock it in place. Once we've established the exact position we need, it's important that you do not move. We've tried to make it as comfortable as possible, and we'll lock you in position only for as long as is necessary. First, though, I need to apply some drops to your eye. They'll cause the pupil to dilate, and also will numb things so that the procedure will be easier for you. Once your eye is ready, I'll tape your eyelid up so that you can't blink. I won't do that until we're ready to shoot the proton beam. I'm just telling you this so you'll know what to expect. Do you understand so far?"

"Yes. I think so. Thank you."

She applied the drops. "Okay, now Jack is behind that little window you are facing. Do you see the end of the proton beam generator?"

"Yes."

"All right. He's ready for us. So you now need to put your chin in this cup."

Mother put her chin in the cup. Then Iris brought the ring down around the top of Mother's head, and asked her to look directly at the little window. Jack made several suggestions to Iris about the positioning of mother's head. Finally, Iris brought out the mask and fastened it to Mother's face so that only her left eye was exposed. Then she tightened the metal ring around Mother's head. She taped my mother's eyelid open, stepped back, and waited. Not more than a minute later, Jack announced that we were done.

"My, that wasn't so bad," Mother said. "Is that all there is to it?"

"Yes, it is." Iris replied. "I'm glad you found it acceptable. Now you have four more appointments each Thursday for the following four weeks at the same time."

◆   ◆   ◆

"Do you mind if I lean back and close my eyes? I am rather tired," Mother said as we pulled out of the parking lot.

"Of course not, Mother. You must be exhausted."

"I have to admit I am," she said. She leaned her head back and closed her eyes. As we arrived back on Cape Ann, she woke up.

"How are you feeling? Any aftereffects?" I asked.

"None that I can see. I'm feeling pretty good."

"Excellent. Well, now you can relax for a week. Get back to your routine."

"Yes. I must say the past couple of weeks have put a crimp in my style. I've not been able to work for my patients as well as I would like. It'll be good to get back to what I'm supposed to be doing."

◆   ◆   ◆

As soon as we were finished with the cyclotron procedures, visits to Dr. Dixon's offices started again. The first was one week following our last visit to Harvard. Dr. Dixon pronounced that the tumor was receding. Each week more progress was reported. Finally, after six weeks, Dr. Dixon announced that the tumor was gone.

As we headed back to Rockport, Mother said to me, "Thank you, dear, for taking care of me during this entire business. I couldn't have done it without you."

"That's what sons are for, Mother. There was no way Barbara and I wouldn't have taken care of you. You know that."

"Yes, I do. But I am so grateful to you and Barbara. I am very fortunate."

We remained silent for the rest of our drive. As we reached our street, I silently thanked God for getting us through this ordeal. In spite of some misgivings about the efficacy of CS, it did seem that we had been led to the right person to take care of Mother's eye, as we had been with Barbara's eye, and even with Mother's hysterectomy. "Can you imagine what it would have been like if they had removed her eye?" I thought.

It seemed that I was always coming back to the idea of being led. My father had been led to speak to an education counselor, which led us to apply to McBurney. I felt I had been led as to what to say at that religious conference at Buck Hill Falls. I was led to blurt out our problem with Carly's adoption agency to a stranger who gave me the answer we needed. There were so many instances in my life of being led.

"But what about the healing thing?" I asked myself as I pulled into our driveway. "I have no answer for that right now. Except to say that Mrs. Eddy condoned having bones set and the taking of morphine to kill pain so one could pray more effectively. Those medical procedures worked in her time. Pretty much nothing else did. What would she have thought of today's medical advances? They certainly have worked for us. No matter, I can't help but feel blessed. Mother's been beautifully taken care of."

I got out, came around the car, and opened the door for Mother. I gave her my hand for support as she pulled herself out. She took my arm, and we walked up the seven steps and through the front door. "I have to admit I am a bit tired," she said. "I think I'll lie down for a while."

MOTHER

On Thursday, April 25, 1996, I found myself in the waiting room of the emergency room at Addison Gilbert Hospital in Gloucester. My mother had complained for several days of extreme pain due to constipation. When I suggested the hospital she responded, "I'll do anything to get relief."

A couple hours later, Dr. David Strong came into the waiting room and asked me to follow him. David was my physician. I had known him for years socially, and I had called on him in rare cases, such as when I had a hernia. Recently he had suggested that it was time for me to have regular check-ups, and I had agreed. I asked him to help Mother since she had no doctor of her own.

He led me to a light box that was hanging on the wall in the hall, stuck an X-ray under some clips at the top and flipped a light switch.

"We found no obstruction but we did find this." He pointed to a small whitish area in the vicinity of my mother's chest.

"What is it?"

"I'm afraid it's cancer."

"Cancer! Is there anything you can do?"

"Theoretically, yes—with a much younger person. But your mother's ninety-three. The chances of success would be quite a bit less than even 50 percent, and the treatment would be very trying."

"Is she experiencing any pain?"

"No. I asked her. It's only the constipation that's been a problem for her."

"What should we do, David? Should we tell her?"

"That's always a difficult question. What it comes down to is, do you want her to start worrying now? Or do you allow her to live her normal life, and wait until she has to come to terms with it?"

"You mean until she begins to suffer?" I asked.

"Well … yes. However, she needn't suffer unnecessarily. We have medications we can give her to relieve any symptoms that present themselves."

"You know," I said, "my father-in-law died here in 1992 of liver cancer. I'll never forget one of the nurses saying how lucky we were that he didn't know about it until the end. Let's not tell her. She's leading an active life."

I wondered to myself: "Am I preventing her from treating herself in Christian Science? Have I any right to do that? Would she have any success? Am I doubting the efficacy of Christian Science?"

"All right," Dr. Strong said, "we've done all we can here. I'll have a nurse explain to you and your mother what needs to be done regarding the constipation."

◆   ◆   ◆

On Thursday, September 12, 1996, Mother and I walked into Dr. Strong's offices.

"Hello Mrs. Ellis, Bob tells me you're having some problems with breathing?"

"Yes. It's very strange. I can't describe it except to say it's a sort of heavy feeling in my chest. And I have this cough every now and then. Bob insisted I see you."

"Well, let me take a listen," Dr. Strong said as he helped Mother climb onto the examining table, and sit on the edge. He asked her to unbutton the top few buttons of her blouse. He then had her take deep breaths while he listened with his stethoscope. "All right, Mrs. Ellis. I think we had better have another x-ray."

After the x-ray was taken, Dr. Strong had us come into his rather cluttered office. "You have a serious condition, Mrs. Ellis. And there's no way to say it other than to tell you that you have a growth in your lung."

"Do you mean cancer?"

"Yes. I'm afraid so."

"Oh dear. Is there nothing you can do?"

"I'm afraid not for the cancer as such, but we certainly can do a great deal to relieve your symptoms."

Mother remained silent for a moment. Then she said, "Do you know how long I have?"

"I really don't, Mrs. Ellis. However, you are otherwise in good shape. So if I had to guess, I'd say you'll be with us for at least several months, even a year."

Mother nodded a brief assent but made no comment.

"In any case," Dr. Strong continued, "we need to be certain that when problems present themselves they will be addressed immediately. The first thing I'd like to do is visit you in your home, see what facilities you have. Will that be all right with you?"

"Oh, yes. That's very kind of you."

"In the meantime, I'm going to write a prescription for some drugs you should have at hand. One will be very helpful for you in overcoming the heavy feeling in your chest. And the other is for the cough," he said as he got up from his chair. We followed. As Mother started to leave his office, David reached out and patted her on the shoulder. She looked at him and smiled. He smiled back. I was close to tears.

◆   ◆   ◆

We drove home in silence. I could only imagine what Mother must have been thinking. Was she laboring over this sentence of death—over finding herself suddenly at the mercy of doctors and drugs?

"She must be praying like hell." I thought to myself. "Knowing that even this suggestion of mortal mind, no matter how severe, can be met. But she's going on ninety-five. She often asks, 'Why am I still here?' Almost all of her friends are gone. 'I have nobody to talk to.' Is it time for her to go? Is that it? Is it a question of time? No, not if CS has anything to do with it."

Mother broke into my thoughts, "Well, there's only one thing I'll ask, Bob."

We were waiting at a red light. I looked across the seat at her and asked, "What's that?"

"I only ask that, as this thing progresses," she pointed at her chest, "I be kept as comfortable as possible."

"You will be, Mother. I promise you. We'll do everything in our power to be certain you are okay."

"Thank you, Dear. I do appreciate everything you've done for me. I am so grateful. I've been beautifully cared for."

"I should have known. No pie in the sky metaphysics. Not at this instant." I thought.

◆   ◆   ◆

Promptly at 11:00 on Saturday morning, Dr. Strong showed up at our home. Mother had her own spacious room with a private bath. We built it for her ten years ago. David looked over her quarters. He recommended we purchase a walker, a portable potty, which could be placed next to her bed at night, and a special grab bar for her to use in her tub. He asked Barbara and myself about our ability to help Mother if and when the need might arise. We assured him that we'd be able to handle things. We also told him about a close friend of ours who had become a companion for Mother, taking her out to lunch and for drives around Cape Ann. He knew Jackie Boyd quite well.

◆   ◆   ◆

On Tuesday, October 16, 1996, Jackie came down the stairs from Mother's room. I was in the kitchen. "I think we need to talk," she said. "Your mother is wonderfully self-reliant. She doesn't want any help unless it's absolutely necessary, takes her own bath, keeps saying she doesn't want to be a 'pain in the neck.' But I can't help but notice that it's getting so she can't be left alone. As far as I can tell, the only time you and Barbara are able to leave here together is when I'm here. Your mother mentioned it."

"She's right. It's not that she demands constant attention. It's just that something might happen. She could fall. She has several times. I know she means it when she says she's afraid she's being a pain in the neck. But what can we do? She's my mother."

"Have you thought about calling Hospice? I've had a couple of patients who made use of them. I don't know how their family would have coped without them."

I called Hospice. A very cordial woman explained to me that, for Hospice to work with us, there had to be a prognosis of no more than six months for Mother to live.

So, to get the help we needed, I had to come to grips with the idea that Mother would not live for more than six months.

"So what do I have to do?" I asked. The woman on the phone put me on hold. Soon, she came back and said that a registered nurse named Kathleen Schroot would come by at nine o'clock tomorrow morning.

At 8:55 the next morning Kathleen Schroot arrived. She sat at the kitchen table, opened her brief case, and pulled out some forms and a pen. "I need to get some information from you before I see your mom," she said. She filled out several forms with Mother's name and address; Barbara's and my names; Jackie's name, schedule, and phone number; Mother's social security number; her physician's name and phone number; and a list of medications prescribed by Dr. Strong.

After writing it all down, she looked at me and asked, "And how are you and Mrs. Ellis coping?"

"Truth be known, it's getting difficult. I mean we have all these medications we have to give Mother. It's hard to know when to give them and how much to administer. And it's getting so we simply cannot leave her alone. We only leave her alone when Jackie's here. I'm getting really stressed, very tired. I'm afraid I've become rather irritable. I know it sounds callous. But I never thought I'd have to care for my mother in this way."

"I understand completely," she said. "I can only tell you that you're not alone. That's why Hospice exists. Now I think I should visit your mother."

I brought her upstairs. Mother was seated in her easy chair, which was a few steps from her bed. Mother had insisted that I have the room straightened up and that she be dressed and sitting in her arm chair for the nurse's first visit. She smiled at Kathleen as they shook hands. Kathleen suggested I go downstairs while she chatted with Mother.

Twenty minutes later, Kathleen came back into the kitchen. "She really is a very nice lady, isn't she? We had a nice chat. She's fully aware of what's going on. And she understands completely about the new level of care we're going to be bringing her. She's glad to know you'll have some relief."

"When can you start?"

"I don't see why we couldn't start right away," she said as she pulled out her calendar. "I can come in next Wednesday and Friday mornings and the following Monday. That can be a regular schedule. Jackie has Tuesdays and Fridays off so I'll have a home-health-aid come in during those times. We also have volunteers who can come in. They can 'baby-sit,' if you will. It will give you a chance to get out of the house for a couple of hours."

◆   ◆   ◆

On Wednesday, November 27, 1996, the day before Thanksgiving, Jeff and his new wife, Magda, were due to arrive at our home from New York. Carly was coming in from Washington College in Maryland. Would this be their last Thanksgiving with their Nana? I knew she would be so glad to see them. Mother desperately wanted to get dressed up, come down from her room, and sit at the table for dinner.

She did still get out of bed on her own these days, for the most part. She could put on her bathrobe, brush her few remaining teeth and her dentures, and sit up in her easy chair to have her late morning breakfast. She tried to read a little, but her eyes had become a problem. Or she watched TV, mostly CNN.

There would be no Hospice assistance on Thanksgiving. But with the family here, we would have no problem.

Mother wasn't suffering unnecessarily. At least she wasn't suffering most of the time. It was all a question of anticipating a problem and treating it before it cropped up. I had never thought that I'd see myself playing doctor, analyzing a patient's needs, and then prescribing and administering medications. They'd never allow that in a hospital, but in the home it was/is the only way. Except for Kathleen, no representative from Hospice could administer the medications. Some of the home health aids and volunteers were registered nurses. But, Kathleen explained, they were not working in our home in that capacity. I just knew insurance was the problem. Nurses were covered by insurance only when they were being nurses, never otherwise, no matter how much more expert they were than I.

We had a supply of syringes, which we filled from a bottle with 1.5 milligrams of morphine. When mother complained of the heaviness, I squirted a syringe into a small cup of fresh orange juice, and she drank it. The juice killed the morphine taste.

The liquid morphine was Kathleen's suggestion. Dr Strong had prescribed two 15 mg pills of morphine each day. The idea was that Mother would stay comfortable without us having to run to her constantly. But it put her into a stupor. Sometimes she didn't know where she was or who I or Barbara were. I thought the cancer was somehow making her lose her mental faculties. Seeing Mother this way was rather frightening. Kathleen recognized that she was getting too much morphine. So she recommended the juice system. Soon, Mother became much more alert.

However, using the juice system meant that someone had to be there to give Mother a dose as soon as she called. Otherwise she would very quickly be in great distress.

Maybe tomorrow, Jeff or Carly could tend to their Nana for awhile. That would be wonderful, though I hated to have them aware of their Nana's condition. She didn't want them to know either. She kept putting up a brave front; even with Kathleen and the volunteers and home-health aids. But Nana's grandchildren did know what was going on. It was just that I doubted that they were aware of the level of care their Nana required these days, to say nothing of what we might be facing down the road.

◆   ◆   ◆

Sunday, January 5, 1997: We made it through Christmas. Carly went back to college, Jeff and Magda back to New York. It was wonderful having them home.

Mother was able to come down for a spell while we opened presents and again later for dinner. But the kids remarked to me how frail Nana looked. They hadn't seen her since Thanksgiving. I saw her every day. Somehow, you don't notice the withering away one day at a time. They were a big help. I'm always amazed at how much Carly and Jeff love Mother. Carly cried a little in the kitchen. She knew. We all knew. It was just so damn hard to come to grips with what was happening upstairs.

◆   ◆   ◆

For the past six months Barbara and I had been planning a six-week trip to Ireland. Everyone told me I should get away for a spell. I couldn't help feeling guilty at the thought. Could I simply leave Mother?

Amazingly, she still is a Christian Science practitioner, and has a wide spectrum of clients who call her for guidance and help.

But now, she is blind in one eye, almost blind in the other, and she mostly lies on her bed because she's so tired. She's unable to sit up for long, yet she still answers the phone and rallies to the needs of her patients. She entertains the nurses when they come to check on her; she still gets up, takes a bath, and gets dressed every day, but she gets exhausted and sometimes goes back to bed. And sometimes, she wrestles over why this "untruth" called cancer is getting her. Then she'll say, "Goddamn it all, why the hell am I still here?"

"It's unbelievably depressing." I kept thinking "The thought of watching my mother die is intolerable. She should be alert and thinking. She is an extremely intelligent, bright, entertaining person. I always thought I would walk into her room one day, find her sitting in her chair with her books in her lap and a slight smile on her face, and she would no longer be with us."

◆   ◆   ◆

Feb. 22, 1997: I brought Mother's pills to her.

"Oh no," she said, "I've felt so much better without the pills."

We had reduced the number due to doctor's orders regarding high blood pressure. And not wanting to aggravate diarrhea (nurse's orders). I assured her that this little blue pill was only to keep her comfortable for the night. She took it and then lay on her right side. I rubbed her back, and she said it felt so good. I told her Jeff was coming home next Monday night to see her. "Oh that's wonderful," she said. Then she said, "I cried a little today."

"You did?"

"Yes, I was alone. It was only a little. I was saying good-bye to everyone."

I made certain she was drifting off to sleep. Then I went to bed and cried.

◆   ◆   ◆

On Feb. 23, 1997, I found myself struggling with role reversal. Everyone had been remarking about it. But the big difference, I said to them, was that a mother cares for her child so willingly because of her sense of wonder and great expectations for that child. But we're waiting for death. Of course, I knew I shouldn't be. Mrs. Eddy tells us: "Life is eternal. We should find this out, and begin the demonstration thereof. Life and goodness are immortal."[1] It was one of Mother's favorite quotes.

◆   ◆   ◆

On Feb. 28, 1997, at 5:00 AM, Mother called out. I went into her room. She complained that she couldn't turn over. Her right arm hurt. She sat up. I gave her some cough medicine as she was coughing a bit. Then I gave her some Tylenol for the pain in her arm. She used the potty and went back to bed. I wondered if she would remember any of it?

It had gotten so I would hear her immediately.

"I am so tired." I said to Barbara.

Later the Hospice social worker and the chaplain both told Barbara to get me away for as long as possible. Jackie, Carly, Jeff, and Magda would take care of Nana. They all practically pushed me out the door. So we went to Ireland. Our original plans were to stay for six weeks. Now I was hoping to stay three. Less than two weeks after we arrived, Jeff called. Dr. Strong was with him. They were in Nana's room. I had better get home right away. We arrived home Friday, March 21 1997. I was practically overcome with guilt when I entered Mother's bedroom. Seeing her curled up on her side in her bed—I didn't recognize her. She had withered down to a tiny shell of herself.

"She must be very close to death." I thought. *"And I went and left her!"*

I held her hand. She was so glad I had come home. She could hardly raise her head. I kissed her on her cheek. "It's all right now Mother. I'm here."

---

1.   *S&H* 246:27

"Thank you, Dear, for coming home," she whispered.

Mother's suffering had become merciless. Carly sat with her during the first week of our trip away, then Jeff came in. God, what saints those two were. And Magda, our new daughter-in-law, she was a saint too. When we left, Mother was sitting up in her chair, eating, taking her blue pill at night and the liquid morphine during the day. She was alert. I spoke to her from Ireland, and she told me how wonderful and devoted Carly and Jeff were.

Jeff had written down the routine he had for Nana. It was very different from the written instructions I gave him before we left. It included a much more stringent schedule of medications. Mother no longer could sit up to drink her morphine/orange juice cocktail, so Jeff squirted two syringes into her mouth simultaneously—one filled with morphine, the other with juice. Trying to ease Mother's pain had become a twenty-four-hour unending vigil.

On Friday, March 28, 1997, Carly arrived home for spring vacation, and Jeff and Magda came up from New York. We were together for one week. The atmosphere in the house was terrible. It was so depressing. God, how I love those children. Carly even climbed into bed with her Nana wanting to comfort her.

On Thursday, April 10, 1997, I was becoming desperate. Mother kept asking "Bobby, how much longer is this going to take?" It was getting so I couldn't stand trying to be the arbiter of how much morphine to give her, how much valium, how much codeine? I had the responsibility for controlling my mother's misery.

On the same day at 5:00 PM, I called Hospice and told them I couldn't handle it any more. Something had to be done to "put Mother out of her misery permanently." David Strong called me back. He would have the nurse come out ASAP and install a morphine pump.

A short while later on that same evening my mom said, "My eyes are stuck together."

"I know, Mother. I am giving you some drops for that."

"Please get me a wash cloth."

I got her a warm cloth and washed her eyes, her face.

"I can't stand the pain," she said. "It's my whole body. You have no idea what agony I'm in."

I took a cloth and folded it up warm and wet on her eyes. It seemed to bring some relief. I gave her some more morphine and some valium. She quieted down. But how much longer could this go on?

I called Hospice again: "I am beside myself," I said. "The pump will arrive at 8:00 PM," was the response.

At 8:00 PM, a new nurse arrived and installed the pump. It was giving Mother a steady stream of morphine through a needle in her thigh.

At 8:00 AM Friday, April 11, 1997, I sat next to Mother's bed. There was a button on the morphine pump, which I was to push if I thought Mother needed more. She must not wake up. Her body was a machine now. It was sucking in and expelling air, but not much was getting into her system. There was no air exchange in her lower lungs.

As I sat and watched this machine that once was my mother, I wondered, "Where is Christian Science? Where is the sense in this literal torture? What is the point of having this mindless growth expanding through a person's lungs? People keep telling me there is a reason. There's some sort of deeper meaning. How can there be any religious, philosophical, physical justification for this?

"Why the hell do we keep on? This human condition is so stupid. What is the point? If ever there was a person who should not have suffered in her death it is Mother. No person has exemplified the truths of Christian Science more than she, with her vision, her spirituality, and her practicality. And this is her reward?—this machine called my mother gasping for air? 'Bobby, please help me! Bobby, how much longer is this going to go on? Bobby, you have no idea how awful this is!'"

I heard myself say out loud, "There is no God."

Noon: Kathleen arrived. She agreed that Mother should go into the hospital. She was comatose with the morphine. She was breathing exactly twelve breaths per minute. The oxygen machine output was as high as I could get it. Her heart was beating a rapid 116 beats per minute. It was trying to get some kind of air out of what was coming in, but it was losing the battle as her lungs were almost gone. However, she didn't know and didn't care—not with that morphine pump performing its magic.

5:00 PM: The Hospice ambulance took Mother to Addison Gilbert in Gloucester. We followed. They told us that hearing is the last sense to go, so even if she was almost totally deaf she still might be aware of what we were doing.

"Are you here, Mother, looking down on me from the ceiling? Have you left that mortal veil? Are you glad it's finally over?"

6:30 PM: We left mother, and went back to the Yankee Clipper for dinner.

7:45 PM: We returned to the hospital. The staff had turned Mother over onto her other side. Someone had combed her hair. But her condition was the same. I tried to put a little water in her mouth. It poured back out. I ran my hand through her hair. Her breathing had become very shallow. "This isn't going to last much longer," I said to Barbara. I leaned over and said into Mother's ear: "I love you, Mother, so much."

We left her at 9:00 PM, went home, and went to bed.

Saturday, 4:00 AM, April 12, 1997: "Mr. Ellis. This is Doctor Ingersoll at Addison Gilbert. I'm calling to tell you your Mother died at 3:45 this morning."

♦   ♦   ♦

Tuesday, April 26, 1997: "Who can find a virtuous woman? For her price is far above rubies. Strength and honour are her clothing; and she shall rejoice in time to come. She openeth her mouth with wisdom; and in her tongue is the law of kindness. She ... eateth not the bread of idleness.... Many daughters have done virtuously, but thou excellest them all.... a woman that feareth the Lord, she shall be praised ... let her own works praise her in the gates."[2]

We were sitting in the Burgess and Mackey Funeral Home in Rockport. Dana Gatlin was reading from the Bible. His wife, Mitzi, would sing the solo. Tears were welling up in my eyes.

Barbara, Jeff, Carly, Magda, my cousin John, and I sat in the front row. Mother had said she wanted no muss or fuss, but we felt we had to have a memorial service. Her body had been cremated. We planned to place her ashes in the Locust Grove Cemetery in Rockport next to Barbara's parents.

The funeral home was packed. I had thought only a few people might attend, mostly fellow members from the Rockport church. But it felt as though the whole town had come out.

"My God, Mother. Do you see all these people?"

Dana read a sermon that he had put together from the Bible and *Science and Health*, just like a Wednesday evening meeting. Mitzi sang "How Lovely Are Thy Dwelling Places" by Brahms, which is in our Hymnal. Bob Littlefield, another good friend from chorus, and one of the finest organists on the North Shore, volunteered to play the organ. He, too, knew and loved Mother.

I hardly heard the rest of Dana's readings. The first citation said it all.

♦   ♦   ♦

Later, on a warm April morning: The sun was shining brightly; the ocean was visible perhaps two thousand feet away. We stood in front of the headstone that

2.   Bible. King James Version. Proverbs 31:10 and following

commemorates my in-laws and soon would commemorate my mother and my father. A small hole had been dug. It awaited the planting of Mother's ashes. Jeff suggested we all hold hands. Carly, Jeff, Magda, Barbara, John, Dana, Mitzi, and I stood in a semicircle around the hole. Someone—I think it was Carly—started reciting, "Our Father, which art in Heaven …" we all joined in. Then Dana started, "The Lord is my Shepherd …" We all followed.

I felt so angry. Earlier Dana had suggested to me that Mother's experience was not unlike Jesus's on the cross; my God, why hast thou forsaken me? He and Mitzi visited Mother a couple of times during the past weeks. She had been Dana's practitioner. They saw what Mother was going through. "Give me a break," was my answer to Dana.

Still, Mother believed in the resurrection and ascension.

An attendant brought the marble urn over to us. Jeff and I struggled with it as we placed it at the bottom of the hole.

I was so relieved that Mother's travail was over. But I was angry—utterly disillusioned. I had always believed in a loving, caring God. But these last six months! We had seen a lot of loving, caring people. But where was God? Would I ever get over it?

IRELAND

In March, 2004, Barbara, I and Mary Higgins, a Rockport Artist and good friend for many years, left Boston's Logan Airport and headed for Ireland.

Six hours later just as the Aer Lingus plane began its descent for Shannon Airport, I collapsed. As soon as we landed, Police and paramedics came on board; customs officials stamped our passports on the plane where I was lying down. The paramedics carried me out to a waiting ambulance. Barbara and Mary sat with me in the ambulance. The paramedic constantly asked, "Are you okay, Robert? "Yes. I'm okay." And I believed I was. Then we arrived at the hospital, and I underwent three hours of tests. There were many nurses, another doctor.

Finally, they said, "We can't find anything. Go home and rest."

On the plane, I had barely heard people talking to me. But I did hear Barbara whispering in my ear: "You are only divine consciousness. You cannot lose consciousness. You are God's perfect child." They were words only a Christian Scientist could have spoken. She was telling me that I could not lose consciousness because, in reality as a child of God, God's consciousness was mine. These words came from my wife who had resigned from the church not long after my mother had died. She had said she was only being a hypocrite when going to church. "I have a doctor. What's the point?"

I, too, had resigned the local church about a year ago. The services had begun to tire me. I could think of no other description. But I did not drop my Mother Church membership. I couldn't quite bring myself to do that. Why? Was I being a hypocrite as well? We both had come to rely on our respective doctors. At the same time, however, it was not unusual for us to quote some CS "truth" to each other from time to time.

In any case, I was so grateful that Barbara was at my side praying. That's what my supposedly non-CS wife was doing. At the very least, it was comforting.

The doctor said we should go home. Home was three hours away in Skibbereen in Southwest County Cork. Barbara and I shared the driving. We made it though we were exhausted. But I felt I had recovered.

We spent the next two weeks touring with Mary whose husband had recently passed away. She wanted to search her roots. Her time with us was a chance for renewal, she said. Seeing the beauty of this land where her grandparents had lived was a spiritual journey.

"I know God has a purpose for me. It's known to God, and revealed to me as I listen day by day. Whoever would have thought it would be possible for me to be able to walk on the very streets my grandparents strode. I never would have thought it possible. Yet here I am. It makes me feel so humble. I am so grateful," she said.

Mary, too, was praying on that Aer Lingus flight. She was a Lutheran. But it is the same God. Isn't it? I recalled my mother kneeling next to Mrs. Farrell all those years ago. "We may pray differently," she had said. "But we are praying to the same God."

Mary stayed with us for ten days. Then our second guest arrived with her husband. She had been Barbara's high school roommate at Daycroft Boarding School—a Christian Science school in Connecticut that our daughter also attended. Barbara and Nellie had been friends for more than fifty years. Nellie made it clear from the beginning of her visit that she had never wavered from Christian Science, not for one instant. She never, ever, had gone to a doctor—not for herself, not for her children.

"There was a time when I was equally firm in my CS," I thought to myself one evening after we had gone to bed. I sat up with a book in my lap. "I once knew, without question, that God existed and that every individual was a pure and perfect child of God. This was not a question of mere faith. I *knew* this. No matter what problem confronted me, I knew that only a *belief* in the reality of mortal mind, of matter, caused the problem. In true reality, there was no matter. God and his spiritual creation was true reality. I knew this deep down in my heart of hearts.

But after Mother's horrible death, I stopped *knowing*. If she had gone peacefully, the way I had always believed she would, that would have been one thing. But six months of pain? Where was God's perfect creation in that?

One could argue that there had been earlier compromises—Mother's hysterectomy and that eye tumor, Barbara's detached retina. But in all those cases we could see God showing us the way. Still, if you listened to Nellie, all this was compromise. We had failed our radical reliance on God. That's what CS calls for, she declared. Those were Mrs. Eddy's words, "radical reliance."[1]

---

1. *S&H* 167:26 The scientific government of the body must be attained through the Divine Mind. It is impossible to gain control over the body in any other way. On this fundamental point, timid conservatism is absolutely inadmissible. Only through radical reliance on Truth can scientific healing power be realized.

"How can you pray effectively for a patient when they are being mesmerized by the idea that medicine is more powerful than God's healing ways?" Nellie had debated earlier this evening. "The Mother Church Board is wrong. They're pandering to the new-agers, trying to appeal to the mind-over-matter idea. That's not Christian Science. It's not a question of mind over matter. It's a question of there being no matter." I closed my mouth when she said that. Nellie was a good friend and would be staying with us for a week. What was the point in arguing?

But Nellie's interpretation of Christian Science teachings did seem extreme to me. Her view might have been correct in earlier decades. But, today, some Christian Scientists would say that each of us has the freedom to work things out for ourselves directly with God. However God leads us, including being treated by a doctor, is each person's own Christian Science demonstration. And some CS practitioners feel free to support their patients if they find themselves under a doctor's care, the way my mother did. In the past, practitioners would drop their patients if a doctor entered the picture.

I couldn't help wondering to myself. Mary Baker Eddy died in 1910. Back then, for the most part, medicine had none of the remedies available that we take for granted today. She had condoned the use of morphine to kill pain so that one could pray more effectively. She also sanctioned having one's bone set by a doctor. I often wondered why these were sanctioned if one was supposed to be radically reliant on God for healing. The answer, it seemed to me, was that these were two areas of medicine that worked in her time. She, herself, had experienced the benefits of morphine as a painkiller.

I had to believe she would have recognized other improvements in medicine as they came along. I didn't believe that seeking some physical assistance along the way toward healing, taking what my mother would have called 'human footsteps,' obviated basic Christian Science. [2]

"You're at it again." Barbara interrupted my thoughts. "You've gone off into another world. I don't believe you've read a single word since you opened that book."

My constant ruminations had become a source of mirth to Barbara. Just before we had left for Ireland, at a party, I suddenly realized everyone was staring at me apparently expecting a response to some question. They all laughed at my embarrassment.

---

2.   For a description of the several ways in which Mary Baker Eddy sanctioned the use of medical assistance see *Open The Doors of the Temple* by Nancy Niblack Baxter.

"He does it all the time," Barbara said, speaking as though I wasn't in the room. "He's always off in some other world pondering some esoteric question."

"So what had you so involved, Bob?" someone asked.

"You really don't want to know."

"Give it a try." someone else said. "You've gotten our curiosity up."

"Okay. If you must know, I've been studying a book that attempts to describe a physical theory that would explain how consciousness works based on quantum mechanics. That's where I was when you guys so rudely interrupted me," I chuckled.

I now said to Barbara: "I was thinking about Nellie." I summarized for her what I had just been thinking to myself. I then said, "I've been led to consider so many philosophical and religious points of view that I have to admit I really don't know where I stand these days."

"About whether or not you're a Christian Scientist?" Barbara asked.

"It goes deeper than that. I've always believed that at its core there is a truth in the Christian Science way of looking at the world. You can't deny the healings we have had and that other people have had, including people outside of CS. We hear reports all the time on the TV of so-called medical miracles. We often hear that people have turned to prayer as a last resort and have been healed. To me those experiences are proof that something is going on beyond any so-called normal physical explanation.

"Remember how enthralled I was with Carl Jung's autobiography and his interest in synchronicity? He saw these seemingly coincidental but meaningful events happening all the time in human affairs. He speculated that they were caused by what he called 'an a-causal-connecting principle.' To me, he was giving a new name to God. He was describing a force that operates independent of any physical cause-and-effect relationship. When I read a couple of other books on synchronicity, I felt that people were beginning to go beyond the myths and to see that there truly is a beneficial Principle operating."

"What do you mean by myths?"

"All cultures, all religions contain in their mythologies elements of the same story—certain universal ideas such as Motherhood, Mother Earth, even Superman. Jung said that these myths are a part of the human psyche. All of these things Jung calls "archetypes" tend to be incorporated in most cultures and religions. And it seems that no amount of scientific discovery is likely to eliminate this need in humans."

"But aren't you always saying that scientific discoveries have freed humans of the very myths you're talking about?"

"Yeah. But I'm no longer certain that's a good thing. Of course, because of scientific advances, we have nuclear research, medical advances, computers, cell phones, the list goes on and on. We even have come to the point where theories are being propounded that attempt to explain God within the framework of quantum theory."

"I hadn't heard that."

"That's what this book I'm reading is about.[3] According to Evan Harris Walker, the author, all creation, including the Big Bang, can be explained in terms of quantum mechanics. God exists. But God is a physical phenomenon. He tries to put a mystical tone on his description, but no amount of invoking the emotions can change the fact that God, which he calls Consciousness with a capital C, is part and parcel, as well as originator, of this physical existence of ours. And the whole idea leaves me feeling empty.

"What I'm getting at, I suppose, is that I can rationalize intelligence with some kind of mathematically defined quantum mechanical process. But how do you calculate a sense of caring? How do you calculate Love? For the most part, the scientific community eschews attempting to come to grips with any kind of metaphysical concept. Any theory of the universe that cannot be mathematically proved or demonstrated by experiment in the scientist's physical laboratory is anathema.

"The problem with that scientifically purist idea is that any so-called truth about the universe has to include all experience, it seems to me. So many people have experienced enlightenment—the sudden dawning of ideas; so many people have experienced physically inexplicable healing; so many people have experienced synchronicity. So many experiences that cannot be explained on the mathematician's blackboard or in the physicists' laboratory. So many experiences, that nevertheless, are real. They happened. To millions of people over the eons. How can we ignore these events when attempting to write a description of the totality of the universe?"

"So you're saying you're still a Christian Scientist at heart, even if not in the traditional sense?" Barbara said.

"There is a core truth, which CS represents, but we have thousands of years of mystical experience that occurred long before Mrs. Eddy. The experience of leaning on what Mrs. Eddy calls "the sustaining infinite"[4] probably is as old as mankind."

---

3.   *The Physics of Consciousness* by Evan Harris Walker
4.   *S&H* vii; 1 To those leaning on the sustaining infinite, today is big with blessings.

"What about before mankind?"

"That is the sixty-four-thousand-dollar question. Are the phenomena of meta-physics purely a product of humankind? I sometimes wonder if most intuition, most listening to God is really a question of allowing oneself to become still enough for that normally inactive portion of the brain to become active. They say some huge percentage of the brain is never utilized. But that doesn't explain syn-chronicity, where two or more individuals coincide in some beneficial way that can't be explained by physical cause and effect. And how about healings caused by the prayerful efforts of people other than the patient?

"But we still have the question you pose. And my suggestion would be that Truth is eternal. All the answers that were ever needed for any solution, all the principles that dictate the operation of the universe, have always existed. Every-thing man needed to know that made it possible to go to the moon existed before the caveman. It required only the passage of time for those ideas to be discovered. There's no such thing as invention. There's only discovery. When my father invented one of his contraptions he simply discovered a way of putting some-thing together. But that *way* always existed. It remained only for him to discover that way. If you study relativity and quantum theory, you begin to get some con-cept of how impermanent time is. The passage of time has nothing to do with the truthfulness and permanence of ideas. Universal Intelligence simply *is*.

"Ideas aren't things that are created and then decay. There is no graveyard where we bury ideas. Granted, many human concepts are set aside. But I'm speaking of those principles that correctly describe the workings of the uni-verse—most of which, I believe, have not yet been discovered."

"But what about your caring God you described?"

"That, I suspect, may reflect a human attribute we have ascribed to God. The human psyche needs to be mothered or fathered. Hence we speak of an anthro-pomorphic Father/God. We listen to Intelligence. We get answers. We feel grate-ful. That tends to support a suggestion of a caring God to whom we should be grateful. This is one place where I think Mrs. Eddy explains it quite well. Her sense of *gratitude* is more a sense of *acknowledging* that God, Mind, Principle is operating in our intelligence here and now and always. Something that we humans seem to forget. Each time we rediscover God's presence, we are grateful, but God was/is, always.

"Human conjecture may, one day, discover the nature of God including the universe. I'd like to think we could look forward to a time when our universe, its origins, and its workings would be embraced in an understanding of one *universal* Mind, Intelligence, Consciousness, whatever you want to call it, which includes all. Wouldn't it be something if mankind could understand and accept such a concept? I know it's a panacea. But it would mean the end of so much strife."

"Man … does not cross the barriers of time into the vast forever of Life, but he coexists with God and the universe,"[5] Barbara quoted from *Science and Health*.

"It's one of my favorite quotes." I said.

◆   ◆   ◆

One week later, Barbara and I returned to Rockport. The flight was uneventful. Soon after our return I saw Dr. Strong. He told me that my experience on the way to Ireland was due to "inappropriate behavior" on my part. He meant that I'd sat upright for long lengths of time, and I hadn't gotten up and moved around, which kept blood from getting to my brain. "That causes us to faint," he said. "It can happen to anyone." More tests and another EKG showed everything to be normal.

◆   ◆   ◆

So what does it all mean—this life I have led, those paths I have followed? What is the meaning of the choices my parents made for me when I was little? What is the meaning of the choices I have made as an adult? What is the meaning of the choices that Nellie might declare caused me to stray from the truth of being? There were so many choices. What impelled me in those choices? Why, for example, did I walk out of that New York State Bar exam and never look back? And why did I make the choices that followed that one? The long and the short of it, I constantly tell myself, is that without making those choices I wouldn't be sitting in this very comfortable house. Most importantly, I wouldn't have my wife of forty-seven years and I wouldn't have my two children, my daughter-in-law, and my grandchildren.

One could argue that I might have followed a career in law, married some other woman, had two other children, and been happy. Problem with that is that my children were adopted. In Carly's case it is not difficult to suggest that she might not have lived were it not for the choices I, and later Barbara, made. Instead, today Carly has her master's degree in early childhood education and

---

5.   *S&H* 266:29 Man is deathless, spiritual. He is above sin or frailty. He does not cross the barriers of time into the vast forever of Life, but he coexists with God and the universe.

teaches in one of the finer school systems in Massachusetts. And who knows where Jeff might have ended up. Today he is a successful commercial artist and photographer. I'll never forget telling him we were so late in having children because we were waiting for him. I truly believed that then about both my children and I do today.

Some would say it's simply a question of chance. I can't accept that. True, I made some crazy choices along the way. Perhaps I wasn't listening properly. But they all became learning experiences. No, I can't help but believe that most of our choices were impelled. Impelled by what? And so my analytical side keeps asking: Well then, what *is* God? What is this apparent force, which appears to act in our lives? Nellie, of course, *knows* what God is. God is Spirit, Mind, Principle, Love, Truth, Soul, Life. Those CS synonyms for God were drilled into my consciousness as they were into hers. But what does it mean to say God is Life? Do we mean the life we see around us? The grass, the trees, the birds, our cats?

Or does it mean that mysterious animating force that is manifested in these life forms? Animating force comes close, I suppose. But, according to CS, what we see with our eyes is not the reality of Life. It is only our limited visualization. It is our illusion. There is a real expression of Life. But we see it only dimly. If we understood the truth about reality we would see the perfect manifestation of the Life that is God.

Is there any sense to this way of looking at things? Any at all?

Barbara's right. I do ponder a lot.

Quantum theory tells us that all subatomic particles, *of which we are made*, are literally ethereal. They have no firm, three-dimensionally observable existence. In fact, they cannot be observed in a physical laboratory in their complete state. Any attempt to observe, say, an electron causes its natural unobservable state to collapse (that's the word physicists use) into only one of the possible states that the particle possesses in its normal every day existence.

Quantum theory also paradoxically tells us that even though nothing can travel faster than the speed of light, pairs of subatomic particles somehow know what each other are doing across vast areas of space *simultaneously*. There is no communication. These particles just "know," *instantly*, what is happening to each other, and they react accordingly. At least one 1990 theory stated that this suggests that our universe is *conscious*.[6] This physical phenomenon also suggests that we are not separate entities existing in individual localities. Rather, because we are made up of these very particles, we are connected to the entire universe.

---

6. *The Conscious Universe* by Menas Kafatos and Robert Nadeau; Springer-Verlag 1990

Albert Einstein's Theory of Relativity tells us that there are no absolutes in this universe of ours except for one. That is the speed of light, which never varies from its 186,000 miles per second. And so, everything else in the universe must adjust itself to that one absolute. That's why astronauts traveling at high speeds age more slowly relative to those of us remaining on the earth. It sounds ridiculous, but it has been proven true. Relativity also tells us that gravity is not a force that *pulls* us toward the center of the earth. Rather it is a manifestation of a geometry of space-time, with four dimensions, which *pushes* us toward the surface. And it says that the concept of time has no meaning in the universe. There isn't even a now. There only *is*.

Chaos theory tells me that if we look deep enough into the most chaotic turbulence we find order.

Hotly debated string theory, which is only a mathematical construct, posits an up to eleven dimension, elemental "vibrating string" (or membrane) without mass and without energy, which is behind each and every subatomic particle in the universe and which dictates the behavior of all matter. One might say all matter, including ourselves, listens to the vibrations of the universe. Some scientists say this theory, which cannot be proven in any physical laboratory, borders on the metaphysical.

Nothing is as it seems. Our mundane, three-dimensional senses deceive us. Physicists agree. When it comes to defining reality, this world of ours is illusory.

So, what is the truth of being? Can it ever be defined?

So many questions remain unanswered for me.

I stand outside at night and look with awe at our Milky Way. I look with awe at my cat as he effortlessly, gracefully, and perfectly lands on the kitchen counter. I think of that golden light I saw in church. I see my wife of forty-seven years absentmindedly smile at me across the room, and I am filled with a great sense of gratitude and love.

Barbara and I have belonged to a large choral group for some thirty-nine years. No matter what we sing I always am carried away by the music. Sometimes, for no apparent reason, I am brought to tears. Or, while I am sitting in my office a Bach cantata can make me stop everything, close my eyes and listen. And the tears can start to flow.

What are these emotions all about? Psychiatrists will tell me, I suppose, that it all has to do with secretions in certain sections of the brain. Maybe so. But what caused the secretions? My experiences are not unique. Carl Jung and many others have enunciated a numinous existence that appears to be inexplicable in physical terms and that all humans share.

Surely, somehow, a satisfactory, meaningful definition of God can come of all these manifestations. Physicists search for their "theory of everything." Surely any meaningful, useful theory of the universe must include the God-side of existence.

Something *is* going on here. Meaningful non-physical events constantly occur. They are a part of the universe just as much as *we* are a part of the universe, just as much as today's inexplicable, paradoxical matter is a part of the universe.

Barbara asked me if I now see myself as a Christian Scientist. No, I suppose not. Not in any formal sense. But I have to give credit where credit is due. Would I have questioned things the way I have over the years if I had not been told from early on that we must not accept at face value matter's claim to reality?

It's true, you know. We can no longer take our normal way of looking at things for granted. Something much deeper, much more grand, and very meaningful to us all is there. If we could only see it.

EPILOGUE

Like so many people of various faiths, I believed that my faith, Christian Science, described the Truth. It was that Truth that healed my nightmares, got me into McBurney School for Boys, led my father to make me take boxing lessons, showed me how to explain Christian Science during that religious conference at Buck Hill Falls, led me to become a staff writer at the *Christian Science Monitor*, brought my wife to me, told me what to say during that awful rainy night in the car with my father, led us through our near bankruptcy and finally to Rockport, made it possible for us to cope after my father's murder, brought us our two children, defended us against that threat to take our daughter away, and led us through mother's battles with cancer until her final months.

No matter how desperate our situation seemed to be we could turn to God for solutions to all our problems. That's how we coped. We turned to our Christian Science God—to Divine Mind, Truth, Love, Principle, Spirit, Soul, Life—that completely spiritual God whose all-inclusiveness, whose infinity made impossible the reality of the material world and all its seeming pitfalls. Through all our trials and tribulations, Barbara and I held fast to our underlying belief that Christian Science described the "truth of being" as my mother used to describe it. The solution to each trial was proof to us of the efficacy of Christian Science, which triumphed in the face of mortal mind's claims of reality.

And Barbara and I were very active in our local church activities as readers, teaching Sunday school, serving on the executive board. There is no denying that Christian Science was an extremely powerful influence in our lives.

Sure, my family made compromises and rationalizations along the way. Sometimes, if I was seriously ill, my mother gave in to my father and I saw a doctor. I had my tonsils out. Later, after I was married I had a hernia repaired. It was so much easier than trying to pray over each condition. We kept these compromises secret from our fellow parishioners in church. There was a kind of hypocrisy in this I suppose. But we knew of other Christian Scientists who had seen a doctor when CS didn't meet their need. They kept their visits to the doctor secret as well. But we knew, and they knew about us. One just stayed quiet about it. We rationalized that we had done the best we could by praying. We told ourselves, "That's all anyone can ask."

Barbara and I also felt that it was a waste of time to spend so much effort praying over a situation that could be handled in such a practical manner by medical experts. That expertise didn't exist in Mary Baker Eddy's time. But it did in our time, and we took advantage of it in those cases where we had not been able to meet our need through prayer.

When we adopted our children, we took them to a pediatrician. The law required the visits since our children were wards of the state for the first year. Since the law required the visits, that made them okay in the eyes of our fellow Christian Scientists. We didn't have to keep the pediatrician a secret. But we welcomed the pediatrician, and continued with him long after the adoptions were final. Barbara and I felt no sense of hypocrisy. We believed fervently that our children were brought to us by God, and we were led through all their and our tribulations by God.

Then, by the time my in-laws died, I began to recognize that I was having to deal with matter in a very conventional way. As I grew older, physical complaints began to surface. I began to see a doctor, and finally began to speak of "my doctor." My in-laws died in the local hospital. There was no conflict in our thought. There was no way CS was going to solve my father-in-law's extremely painful liver cancer and my mother-in-law's congestive heart failure.

Still, after their funeral, Barbara and I went back to church, and my mother remained very active in the Rockport church and as a Christian Science practitioner. Mother seemed to me to be the epitome of the perfect Christian Scientist. For more than sixty years since my birth, Mother had never seen a doctor nor been in a hospital except to visit her patients. Mother always stuck by her patients when medical care became necessary, unlike most Christian Science practitioners who believed Christian Science and medicine couldn't possibly mix. She maintained a very successful Christian Science practice, was very active in church activities, and read and served on the executive board. At that time, she was in her early nineties, and she appeared to be thriving.

Then her body started to break down. We rushed her to the hospital when she started to bleed uncontrollably. She had an emergency hysterectomy that same day. A huge cancer was removed. But she came home after three weeks and resumed her practice of Christian Science. We had done what had to be done. God, Barbara and I said to ourselves, had directed us. I entertained the notion that this was a rationalization. But Mother had put herself completely in our hands, and we wouldn't have done otherwise.

We were cautioned that the surgeons couldn't be certain that they had gotten all of the cancer. We assured ourselves that Perfect, Infinite, Divine Mind, Divine

Love did not allow room for anything but a complete healing. We were certain that there couldn't possibly be any more cancer. We were grateful to God that once again we had been led to the right people for Mother's problem.

Then the ophthalmologist found the tumor in Mother's eye. That resulted in those weekly trips to Boston and the cyclotron radiation treatments at Harvard. The tumor shrank away. Once again we were grateful that God had led us to the doctor at Massachusetts Eye and Ear Infirmary. Was this a rationalization? The ophthalmologist had said normal treatment was removal of the eye. I couldn't accept that notion so I had responded, "How about removal of the tumor?" He responded that he knew of one doctor who might be able to help. Had Divine Intelligence spoken through me? Or was this simply the logic of events? I chose, in that moment, to believe the former.

Through all of these events I was convinced that the Christian Science God of Mind, Principle, Life, Spirit, Love, Truth was the only definition of God that made sense. I fully believed that I was a human being *only in my own belief.* In the reality of Christian Science, I was made in the image and likeness of Mind, of Principle, of Spirit, of Truth. It was my job to hold to that truth about myself, and in so doing, I would overcome the obstacles that mortal mind—my human mind—kept putting in my way.

Then came my mother's unbelievably painful, heart-wrenching, six-month battle with lung cancer. The diagnosis. The inexorable spreading of the cancer from a small spot to her entire lungs. Our having to decide on the doses of morphine; the doses of codeine; the doses of valium. Her constant cries, "You have no idea what agony I'm in. How much longer is this going to last? Why am I still here?" Her telling me near the end that she had "cried a little last night. It was only a little. I was saying good-bye to everyone." Finally, the morphine pump.

Mother was almost ninety-five when she died. It was not her death that I objected to. It was the way of her death for which I could find no Christian Science or any other rationalization. Thousands of people go through similar experiences every day. Where is their God in their final days?

I came close to concluding that there is no God. I even said so at Mother's bed-side. And I never went back to a church service.

◆   ◆   ◆

And so here's where I am today. I am writing a book in which I'm trying to make sense of my faith. As the writer of this book, I have been able to become an observer. At times, during the process, I have felt like the proverbial fly-on-the-wall. I find myself wondering, "Did that really happen? Did my father really run out into that dark rainy night? Did I really talk him into coming back home?" I have to tell myself, "Yes. These events really did happen. And you are a product of all that has happened."

I always acknowledged my mother's profound faith and influence on me. But it took the writing of this book to recognize my father's way of thinking and the great influence he had on me. I only regret that I never could tell him how important he was to me. I'm convinced it is his curiosity about how things work that lives in me and forces me to keep asking "Does God exist? And, if so, what is God?" Today those are the great questions for me.

Of course, it was what I saw as the failure of the God of Christian Science in Mother's great time of need that forced me to question any existence of any God. But I also look at the world at large—the political and religious strife, the rapes, murders, torturings, genocides —and ask how can any definition of God of any faith be rationally defended.

Then I see so many individuals finding comfort in their faith just as I did in mine. And so I return to my own experience to see if any God concept makes sense to me.

I first look at the world around me. There is something awe inspiring about the world in which I live. I feel the transcendent at work in the Bach cantata that brings tears to my eyes; in the choral works that Barbara and I participate in where we fill a hall full of people with the sounds of Handel, Verdi, Bach, Brahms. I see Intelligence in the activity of nature; the bumblebee buzzing around the flowers in our garden; the ants building their ant hills; the beetles going about their business; the spider's web especially after the dew has fallen and droplets cling to it. Nature displays the most wonderful, seemingly chaotic symmetry all around us. And then there are the sounds of the songbirds singing, the crows cawing, the seagulls crying, squirrels chattering, owls hooting, crickets cricketing.

Do I see a God who has created all these creatures and sounds? No. I accept that all of today's creatures—including man—have evolved, and that evolution has occurred according to scientifically accepted processes of natural selection and mutation. But I do see a *Life force*. The story of life on this earth is that of life forms adapting to adversity and surviving and developing. Think of the tree that insists on growing back after being cut down. Think of the bacteria who adjust to antibodies in order to survive much to our consternation. Think of all the examples of mankind rising above adversity.

But experiencing the transcendent, imbibing in it, dwelling in the sense of well being that comes from these experiences seems to not be enough for me. It's too visceral. I need to find the rational side. I seem to be unable to stop myself from asking, "Where does this sense of the transcendent come from?"

Could the answer lie within my own personal experience? I cannot deny the countless times that I have benefited from a sense of direction that came from some place other than my brain. What, I ask myself over and over, was at work during all those experiences. Perhaps the most amazing experience occurred when the adoption agency was threatening to remove our daughter from our home. How do you explain Barbara's frantic telephone call to me exactly when I was calling on a customer whom I did not know but who turned out to be a psychiatrist? She saw a look of distress on my face as I returned from the phone. For some reason, she asked if there was anything she could do. Why did she ask me? She was a customer. She had no reason to interfere in my troubles. But something made her ask. And what made me blurt out our troubles to this stranger? This woman whom I did not know gave us the answer we needed to resolve our problem. There is no logical way of explaining this chain of events. What was going on here?

Thousands of people have written about similar experiences. How do you explain the logic of such events? The answer is that you don't. There is no apparent logical or causal connection involved except perhaps in something that transcends human logic. Carl Jung identified such events as examples of what he called "synchronicity"—events that he said were not coincidence but the manifestation of an "a-causal connecting principle." In other words, some kind of non-physical, non-logical, all-encompassing force is at work.

Then there's what I can only describe as the sense of a *presence,* which I have experienced. When I felt that sense of peace before I went out to start reading at that church service and I saw everybody and everything bathed in that mysterious light, I felt a palpable presence. It surrounded me and warmed me without any heat. When I kneeled and prayed during a Christian Science communion service, that same palpable presence surrounded me. Even as early as when I had those nightmares, that presence was there. Whenever and wherever I stopped stewing in my own thinking and finally let go and relaxed and allowed the answers to flow, I felt that presence. What was that presence I felt?

Then there's the question of the root source of creativity. Those who are researching the human brain have found no answer to the source of creativity in the brain. So where does creativity come from? I used to ask my Sunday school students to think of the scientists at NASA who figured out how to fly the astronauts to the moon and back. I asked them whether the physical principles employed in that endeavor had been invented by the scientists or had been discovered. Had they existed through all time from the beginning of the universe some fourteen billion years ago and perhaps before? Or had they suddenly been created? Invariably the answer had to be that they were discovered. They had always existed. They only awaited the development of human intelligence to the point where mankind could receive and understand them. Did Mozart create his symphonies out of whole cloth? Or were his creations only awaiting his genius? Do compositions as yet unheard by us exist today?[1]

I believe that they do. I believe works of art, which the artist never dreamt of, exist now. I believe that everything we need to know to solve all our problems here on this earth exists now in a realm of infinite, timeless, universal, palpable Intelligence.[2]

Scientists are predicting that within twenty to thirty years, thanks to the current digital revolution and especially developments in artificial intelligence, we will know so much more than we now know. A type of superintelligence will rule.[3] We will be able to process information trillions of times faster than we can today, they say.

I ask myself: "Well, then, will the answer to the creativity, the synchronicity, the presence questions lie within the newfound power of human intelligence that is being predicted? My gut tells me no. That would suggest that all answers are to be found individually in one's brain, or in the artificial intelligence of some machine, or in a combination of the two. And I simply can't believe it. No matter how fast and sophisticated our thinking may become, I see no way for greater

---

1.   Nobel Laureate Eric Kandel was interviewed on NPR regarding his work on memory loss. He reported promising possibilities for treatment in the very near future. I sent him an e-mail in which I asked: "Can you explain the revelatory inspiration we all experience from time to time?…Is this strictly an internal, within the brain function? Or do you acknowledge the possibility of something else going on outside of individual consciousness—some kind of universal consciousness or intelligence." Dr. Kandel responded "…we do not have meaningful answers for…the core of creativity."

2.   This sounds somewhat like Plato's concept of eternally existing patterns or forms which are reflected imperfectly in the material world—a concept not unlike that of God's perfect reality as defined in Christian Science. But my concept goes more to the source of our answers to our problems, to defining that to which we listen when we pray, to that which led me and mine.

3.   See Ray Kurzweil: "*The Singularity is Near.*" Neil Gershenfeld: "*When Things Start to Think.*"

human/cyborg intelligence to explain the transcendent, the creative, the sense of being led, the synchronistic I have experienced.

Rather, I believe that we are on the brink of discovering scientifically that the universe is Conscious and that this timeless, universal, infinite Intelligence is at work here and now and universally. We are inextricably united with this Intelligence just as we are with the universe. This Consciousness, this Intelligence, working in and through us, explains the healing, transcendent, and creative in our lives. This is the God upon which I and my family have relied through all these decades.

I have left Christian Science behind—that faith that used to be my whole world. I mostly rely on medicine to help me with any physical ailments that come my way. Undoubtedly my sense of infinite Intelligence sounds a lot like the Divine Mind of Christian Science. And I suppose we are speaking of the same thing. But I do not accept the idea that matter is just plain unreal. Rather, I now revel in the beauty that is revealed to me in the wonders of our natural world. And I see divine Intelligence permeating all matter—all existence. And I do turn to divine Intelligence for guidance. I do that all the time. The idea that divine Intelligence is always with me never leaves me.

I have to admit that it was difficult for me to leave the Christian Science church behind. My faith was so important to me when growing up and in my adult life. But I really had no choice. The Christian Science organization, with its Church Manual written by Mary Baker Eddy before she died in 1910, remains locked into a dogma, which, in my experience, allowed for very little exploration outside of the "authorized" literature of the church. If it wasn't available at the Christian Science Reading Room it probably wasn't accurate.

It's too bad. I feel I have grown tremendously as a result of my explorations of realms of thought I never would have dreamt of studying thirty years ago, even to the extent of bringing me back to the basics of my own faith but without feeling restricted by dogma.

I suspect that it is Christian Science, with its vision of only the good and the beautiful, that prepared me to experience the transcendent. I fully acknowledge that Christian Science as my mother taught me along with my father's instruction and his life caused me to look at the world very differently from the way most folks do. I try to never accept anything at face value. Because I have been willing to constantly explore outside of the box in which I was raised, I have met people, had experiences, and been exposed to ideas and cultures I never would have dreamt of. And that exposure has caused me to gain a sense of love for all of my fellow men and all creation.

How many other people of all kinds of faiths from fundamentalist Christians to fundamentalist Muslims, from Hindus to Buddhists, from Protestants to Catholics have not allowed themselves to explore, How many have failed to widen their vision and maybe see and respect other peoples' points of view?

Back when we were seeking the right high school for me, my mother—that fully committed Christian Science practitioner—said to me, "There are several Christian Science schools we could send you to where you would live in an atmosphere of nothing but Christian Science. But, Bobby, there's a whole world out there that you need to know about."

My learning experience has been wonderfully stimulating and fun. If these past years of evolution in scientific and religious thinking are any example, I can only marvel at the possibilities for the future. We're going to see great strides take place, points of view forced to change, cherished beliefs severely challenged. And I'm looking forward to seeing how my own understanding will be challenged and forced to change in the coming months and years.

978-0-595-45627-7
0-595-45627-8

Made in the USA
Middletown, DE
12 March 2020